LAY IT DOWN

LAY IT DOWN

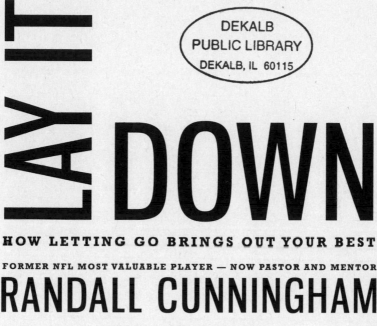

HOW LETTING GO BRINGS OUT YOUR BEST

FORMER NFL MOST VALUABLE PLAYER — NOW PASTOR AND MENTOR

RANDALL CUNNINGHAM

WITH TIM WILLARD

WORTHY

PUBLISHING

Copyright © 2013 by Randall Cunningham

Published by Worthy Publishing, a division of Worthy Media, Inc., 134 Franklin Road, Suite 200, Brentwood, Tennessee 37027.

HELPING PEOPLE EXPERIENCE THE HEART OF GOD

eBook available at worthypublishing.com

Audio distributed through Brilliance Audio; visit brillianceaudio.com

Library of Congress Control Number: 2012956456

For foreign and subsidiary rights, contact Riggins International Rights Services, Inc.; rigginsrights.com

Published in association with Ted Squires Agency, Nashville, Tennessee

Published in association with ChristopherFerebee.com, Attorney and Literary Agent

ISBN: 978-1-61795-127-5

Cover Design: Christopher Tobias, Tobias' Outerwear for Books
Cover Image: Omar Gomez
Interior Typesetting: Susan Browne Design

Printed in the United States of America

13 14 15 16 17 CGFF 8 7 6 5 4 3 2 1

To my wife, Felicity; son Randall II; and daughters,
Vashti, Grace, and Sophia. To my aunt Nettie and our
baby boy Christian—whom we miss so much and will
see again when we meet up in heaven. And to all those
who have lost loved ones along the way . . . I pray you
will use this book to receive your long-awaited healing.
Please lay it down and give it to our Father in heaven.

CONTENTS

INTRODUCTION
PLAYING THROUGH THE PAIN

THE POWER OF "WHAT IF . . . ?"

Fractures well cured make us more strong.

—RALPH WALDO EMERSON

What if I told you that you were about to face severe pain? Gut-wrenching, life-altering, game-changing pain? What if I told you your reaction in that moment had the power to shape the rest of your life for good or bad?

Our immediate decisions in life determine what path we will take or how far we will veer from it. When I played quarterback in the NFL I was paid to make quick decisions. I would break the huddle, approach the line, and look at the defense. I had seconds either to run the play that was called or to audible to another play—one I thought would work better given the defense at that moment.

I barked out the cadence, the center hiked the ball, and I ran the play, handing it off or dropping back to pass. When the play finished, the offense headed right back to the huddle and I'd give them another play. We had plays for every situation—short yardage, long yardage, goal line, everything. And we kept calling plays until we reached our goal: the end zone.

What happened in those seconds before a play is a lot like what happens in life. We all approach the line of scrimmage every morning. We head out to work or school and we read the defense. *What is life going to throw at me today?* we ask ourselves. Then we run our play. We perform in a meeting or we begin a new project, and we respond to criticism or praise, taking what-ever comes our way.

But sometimes the defense gains the upper hand. We lose our job or hear that so-and-so got the promotion we were sure was in the bag for us. We find out our spouse is having an affair. We lose someone we love to cancer. In football we call these moments sacks or tackles behind the line of scrimmage. These plays set us back. And if we let them get too much into our head, we soon find ourselves punting the ball to the other team. We play our own prevent defense. We live in that defeated moment, knocked down and never really recovering.

I've been tackled by some of the biggest and fastest men in sports. And there were times when I wanted to go back to the locker room and ice down early. But here's the thing: getting the snot knocked out of you on the football field or the field of life is a defining moment. It's a chance to ask yourself, *What if I get back up? What if I face this fear? What if I refuse to let the defense see me wince in pain?* It's that "what if" moment that can define the rest of your life.

A couple of things happen in that moment. First, you have to absorb an enormous amount of pain—the kind of pain that makes you feel like you're about to crack in two. The pain says, "Don't get up. Just lie here awhile." Pain's voice is loud, perhaps the loudest voice you'll hear in your life. Many people give in right there. When they feel the pain, they hear its voice and walk off the field.

The second thing that happens in that moment is your mind and soul become tethered to doubt, anxiety, apprehension, and fear. The reality of the hit makes your head ring and immediately your mind begins to bend inward. You start seeing the fight as pointless. The game is over, right?

Defeat, whether in life or in a game, doesn't happen when the final horn sounds. It happens when your opponent takes you mentally out of the game. Where the mind goes, the body follows. When that hit comes to you, what will you do? If it's already come to you, what have you done in response?

So many people think that when life comes at us hard and knocks us down, that's all we're destined for: a life of hard knocks. Not so! It's the hard times that can render us useless, forever on a downward spiral . . . or propel us forward. We can give up, or we can stand up and determine in our mind and soul that we will go back to the huddle and run another play. Legendary Green Bay Packers' coach Vince Lombardi said it well: "The greatest accomplishment is not in never falling, but in rising again after you fall."

This book looks at that moment just before we rise or decide to stay down. When the unthinkable happened, I faced such a time. I was forced to make the toughest decision I've ever had to make in my life. I had to lay down the pain of my situation and decide to face another day.

What if I told you there was hope beyond your trials? What if I told you that life was meant to be lived in abundance and that there's a way to haul yourself up after tough times and keep moving? Would you listen to my story? Would you be willing to lay down your pain and get in the game?

If so, then read on.

YOU'RE NOT THE STARTER

PUTTING YOUR LIFE INTO PERSPECTIVE

Disappointment is the gap between
expectation and reality.

—JOHN MAXWELL

In 1996 I quit football. I'd been with the Philadelphia Eagles for a number of years, but I was done. I never wanted to play football again.

Though I look back now with fondness on my time in Philadelphia, most sports analysts would say it was an eleven-year roller-coaster ride—so much good, so much of the unexpected, and even times when we experienced the unthinkable. For the most part those years allowed me to get into contact with who I was supposed to be as a man in this life. But the later years actually allowed my joy and love of football to depart from me. It was humbling to realize that I was no longer wanted as a starting quarterback when no one invited me to join them for the 1996 season.

So I returned to Las Vegas, the city of my alma mater, the University of Nevada, Las Vegas (UNLV), and started my own tile business—Custom Marble and Granite Accessories. For a year I worked with my laborers, experiencing the rigors of real life on my hands and knees, cutting rock and making marble and granite countertops. It was a rewarding experience. I loved handling the raw materials and observing how they took shape during the refining process. I grew to understand contentment during that year away from the game I had loved. I learned to take nothing for granted, to cherish all the little moments of life as much as the big moments.

But many people kept asking me, "Hey, Randall, when are you coming back?" I felt a prompting to seek God's will for what was next in my life. I was content to keep at the tile business. But did God want me to get back into the game?

To be honest, I didn't want to play football anymore. So I prayed very specifically that God would make it clear if he wanted me to go back to the NFL: "Lord, I don't know if I'm supposed to play, but whatever your will is . . . I'm ready for it. If you want me out there, God, you're going to compel teams to call me. I'll go back if you want me to go back—but if you leave it up to me, God, I'm not going back."

The calls started coming. First Jeff Fisher, who was then coaching the Tennessee Titans. Then Mike Ditka in New Orleans.

I dropped down on my knees. "Okay, God. I see that you want me to go back. I'm not sure why you want me there, but I'll go because you want it to happen. I'll go back, not because I want to, not because I want a Super Bowl ring; I'll go back to see what it is you want me to do."

I received clear direction from God to go back into football, and I signed with the Minnesota Vikings. I was there to back up Brad Johnson, but in my second year playing with the Vikings I received my shot to be a starting quarterback once again. Brad fractured his right leg in the second game of the 1998 season against St. Louis. I came into the game and threw the winning touchdown. The scoreboard read 38–31.Victory!

We lost only one game the whole regular season.

What a whirlwind. There I was, a thirty-five-year-old, once-retired, backup quarterback, slinging bombs down the field to rookie Randy Moss, who would become one of the best receivers of all time. I ended up receiving league MVP honors and had the best year of my career. I threw for 34 touchdowns and only had 10 interceptions. My passer rating was 106, which was a Minnesota Vikings record. Our offense set the single-season scoring record with 556 points scored. (That record stood until the Patriots broke it in 2007, scoring 589 points with—guess who?—Randy Moss. I was not surprised.)

In the world of football, it was a great year. And for me personally? I called it a blessed year.

But the season ended in disappointment. There we were, the highest-scoring offense in the history of the game, watching Morten Andersen, placekicker for the Atlanta Falcons, dash our Super Bowl dreams with an overtime field goal in the NFC championship game. It was a crushing blow for a football player.

Prior to the end of that season I'd been rewarded for my offensive performance with a five-year, $30.5-million contract, even though I told the Vikings I only wanted to play one more year. But after the season, things began changing on the team, beginning with the loss of our offensive coordinator, Brian Billick, who took the head coaching job with the Baltimore Ravens. He was the brains behind our offense.

The Vikings headed into the 1999 season with a new offensive coordinator, Chip Myers, who had been promoted from wide receivers coach after Billick's departure. Things were going as normal until Chip died unexpectedly of a heart attack right before the season. We didn't know what was going to happen after that. We were mourning the death of a great coach and friend. We didn't know who the offensive coordinator was going to be. We scored points, but not like we had in the past. Overall, we weren't firing on all cylinders. We struggled.

The NFL is a "What have you done for me lately?" league. It only took until halftime of the fifth game of the season for Coach Denny Green to bench me. Near the end of the season, however, they asked me to start again, but with a pay cut. Nine months after receiving a thirty-million-dollar contract they wanted me to willingly give up some of it. I said, "Thank you, but no. I'm going to honor my contract." I was due one million dollars after the season, which they paid me. But then they released me.

Then the Dallas Cowboys picked me up for the 2000 season. Jerry Jones said, "Randall, you don't have to worry about being the starting quarterback. We have Troy [Aikman]." So I thought

I was headed to the Dallas Cowboys to back up Troy. This was around the time when Troy endured a string of concussions. They wanted someone ready in case he received another one. I was happy to oblige.

I was a Dallas Cowboy—the Super Bowl–winning Dallas Cowboys. I thought, *I'm backing up Troy Aikman and I'm a teammate of Emmitt Smith, Darren Woodson, and "Rocket" Ismail.* I could not have planned it any better.

Then the unthinkable happened: Troy received another concussion. I replaced him. Now I was really living the dream, right? Wrong. Almost immediately I pulled my hip flexor and was out. That was the extent of my shining career as a Dallas Cowboy: a 1–2 record, 849 passing yards, 6 touchdowns to 4 interceptions.

Not quite like I planned it. I went from the highest-scoring offense in the league to injured backup to Troy Aikman.

Still, at the end of the season Jerry informed me it was possible that Troy might not return to play ball. There was an indication he might have to consider retiring because of the concussions. Jerry told me he wanted me to be their starting quarterback.

So I researched starting salaries, and my wife, Felicity, and I bought a place in Dallas. *Hey, here we go*, I thought. *We're going to finish out my career here in Dallas with the Cowboys.* I could almost see myself riding off into the Texas sunset (minus the cowboy hat and spurs).

But then Jerry called me again and explained that they were having salary-cap issues and that Troy wasn't done yet.

One minute Felicity and I were purchasing a home in Irving, Texas . . . and the next minute my good friend Brian Billick, who at that time was head coach of the Baltimore Ravens, was calling me.

"Randall," he said. "Come on over to the Baltimore Ravens."

I thought, *Wow. The Ravens just won the Super Bowl. This could be a great opportunity.* The Ravens had the best defense in the league. Ray Lewis was there, and Brian Billick had been my offensive coordinator when we broke the scoring record in Minnesota, so I'd be hooking back up with that kind of offense. What an opportunity!

"Yes, I'll come."

So in 2001 I became the backup to Elvis Grbac. I chose to wear the number 1 because I was going to play only one more year. I started just two games with the Ravens that year, but we won both games.

I finally retired from football in 2002—for good this time—as a Philadelphia Eagle once again. I'm very proud of that fact. When I retired from the game I was the all-time leading rusher at the quarterback position with 4,928 yards on 775 attempts. That record stood until 2011.

ANOTHER PURPOSE

Some people ask me if I'm disappointed with how my football career unfolded during those difficult few years. After all, I had just set league records with the Vikings and barely missed the Super Bowl. What was it like to go from such a high place of success in Minnesota to holding a clipboard in Dallas, then playing, then getting injured?

It's a fair question. By the world's standards, perhaps, I was being treated unfairly—inadequately rewarded for my accomplishments. Fate was having a laugh at my expense as I watched from the Dallas sideline.

But to me, that kind of life vision is limited. It places too much stock in the tangible, measurable things in life and not enough on the things that really matter, like the heart and soul of a person. Accolades aren't worthless by any stretch, but they are not the sum total of a person. There's always something going on behind the scenes. In our media-saturated culture all the fans see is a player like me getting shipped out of town to another team and riding the bench or getting injured. But that's only a fraction of life for that individual.

Don't get me wrong: moving from city to city with your family is no small task, and that kind of lifestyle takes its toll. But

I didn't sit around and mope because I felt I was entitled to more in Minnesota. My life didn't end when I was injured in Dallas. I was living my life off the field. And some great things were happening.

During that time my first son, Randall II, was born and then we were blessed with my first daughter, Vashti. I was in a new chapter of life: I was watching the birth of my children. I was watching them crawl around in their diapers. I was watching them grow up. You don't get to replay that down, if you know what I mean. You only get one chance to be with your family, and I wanted to make the most of it. Felicity and I were growing closer as we experienced the fun and crazy world of parenting.

My football career was incredible. It afforded me the freedom and resources to chase after my passions wholeheartedly. For that, I'm thankful. But there is life after the NFL, as so many players find out the hard way. I'm often asked if I regret not getting to or winning a Super Bowl—the crowning achievement for any player. Early in my career I might have answered differently. But I can tell you with confidence now that it doesn't bother me.

We're not defined by singular events in our lives. We're defined by the entirety of our lives—lived to the fullest. My personal faith in God views a life well lived as one that brings honor and glory to him. What I do and the reason I do those things are directly related to making God proud.

Life will shift and change like a quarterback calling an audible at the line of scrimmage—there may be maneuvers and hits that catch us off guard. Our response in that moment is key. Do we freeze at the line and let life barrel through us? Or do we take the shift in stride and make a play?

Losing my job in Minnesota was a shift. Likewise, going to Dallas looked like a great opportunity. But neither panned out professionally. Instead, there was something waiting for me *beyond* the supposed disappointment of those opportunities.

When I retired in 1996, I had begun a small Bible study I hosted at my house. I kept up with that on an interim level; whenever a season ended I'd return to the Vegas area and pick up the Bible study, and all the people involved would return as well.

With that in mind, one day I was talking with the chaplain at Dallas and asked him if I could start a Bible study with some of the guys on Mondays before practice. I wanted to go through the book *The Man God Uses* by Henry and Tom Blackaby. He smiled and told me that he'd been praying for a player to step up in that role and lead a study for the players. It was the beginning of my mentoring young players.

Here I was thinking I was in Dallas to be the backup to Troy Aikman on "America's Team," but God showed me that he had other plans. He wanted to raise me up among my peers to lead them in spiritual matters. What an honor! What a responsibility!

PRIORITIES

People often ask me what I think of the Tim Tebow experiment with the New York Jets. I don't comment at all on Tebow as a quarterback or his skill set or anything like that. I'm not looking at that. I'm looking *beyond* that. What's God doing with Tim? Why would he place him with the Jets when he might have been a perfect fit with the Broncos? I don't know if many in the public will ever understand what Tim's true impact is on society. But I firmly believe that it will be seen in the men he encourages through his involvement in their lives.

That's what was going on with me in Dallas. How could I have seen that when I retired in 1996? There's no way I could have. I had to trust God, lay down my own selfish desires, and venture into unknown waters to find out firsthand what God wanted from me. When my faith began to grow, I released the things that used to be important to me: the drive for success and the desire to do whatever I wanted to do at my own leisure (something that simply isn't possible if you want to make it as a new dad).

As I released those things, I could see myself growing as a man. Yes, I was a professional athlete. But as my career neared completion I transitioned into being a new father, a better husband, and a community leader who *lived* in the community.

I had things I wanted to do and my own ideas for life after

football. But I found out that those notions did not align with God's plan for me. So I laid down my own desires to see what God desired for me. It turns out he gave me success in Minnesota but then gave me arguably greater success in Dallas. My impact that year was not on the football field but in the lives of those men I studied with and mentored. A few years later, that small Bible study in my home grew to become Remnant Ministries, the church I now pastor in Las Vegas.

Maybe it's difficult for a fan to understand, but this is what I tell folks in my church and the young athletes I mentor: get your priorities in order. If my life rested on what I did on the field, then I'd be in trouble. But it doesn't—thank God! That record-setting year in Minnesota was sweet. And that's part of what made the journey so special. But that was not my treasure. In the end I found contentment and purpose because I knew my life did not belong to me. It belonged to God.

This perspective may surprise some people. Sacrificing what we want to do in life for a greater purpose goes against our natural tendencies. In football you're lauded as a player when you have singular vision and strive to be the best—the best of the best—and to win a Super Bowl. It's not that I didn't want to win a Super Bowl, but those goals and aspirations are not life-or-death situations. They're temporary accomplishments. When I came back from retirement I was content to be the best I could be, to strive for excellence, and to accept whatever success or failure came my way.

When our priorities are set in the right place, we don't give up when something bad happens to us. After many years away from football, I would experience that firsthand.

CHAPTER 1
REFLECTION QUESTIONS

*Has there ever been a time when you ended up in a place
or situation you didn't want to be in? Perhaps a lost job, a
difficult relationship, or a frightening situation? What was your
experience? How did you make it through that experience?*

———

*Detail a time in your life when you had a negative
experience that ended up turning into a positive one.
What doors opened for you because of it?*

———

*What are your life priorities? Are they the right ones? Are there any
you believe should be changed? If so, which ones should they be?*

———

2

THE BIGGEST HIT I EVER TOOK

THE DAY THAT FOREVER CHANGED ME

Success is determined not by whether or not you face obstacles, but by your reaction to them.

—BEN CARSON

It was late afternoon on June 29, 2010. I was on my way back from the airport. Everything about the day was typical. I had taken a trip to California to have my body checked out for my NFL insurance plan. It was hot that day, about 111 degrees in Vegas. I was on my normal route from the airport. I couldn't wait to see my family.

But when I drove down the road to my house and turned into my driveway, I knew something was wrong. I'm used to seeing cars in front of the house—Felicity is always having someone over from church—but this was different.

The cars out front did not belong only to our friends. There were police cars—and also a coroner's car. The moment I saw those vehicles, my heart paused and a feeling of numbness came over me.

For some strange reason, I knew this wasn't about my aunt Nettie—our sweet aunt who was to be at my house that day. Somehow I knew that it was my youngest son, Christian. And I knew it had to do with the pool and that he had fallen in. I can't explain that sense of knowing, but that's where my mind and my heart went.

I knew that some tragedy had befallen my youngest son.

When I walked into the house, my oldest daughter, Vashti, was the first to approach me. She said, "Daddy, I'm so sorry. I'm so sorry!"

Then Randall II walked up to me and I could see that he wanted to hug me. Gracie—my youngest daughter at the time—too. I knew something was wrong. My wife wasn't around, but thank God Aunt Nettie was on hand, although I think she was in shock at that point. There were other people in the house as well; they were all trying to figure out the situation. I felt like I was a visitor on a movie set, watching everyone around me doing their jobs without even noticing me nearby. There I was, the father and husband and head of the house, walking in and finding police officers. It looked as though people didn't know what to do or what to say.

The immensity of the moment was coming together right in front of me and it was staggering. The shock was so thick in the air at that point, I could feel it drape over my whole body.

Finally, a police officer came up to me. "Mr. Cunningham, can we talk to you in a private room?"

I said, "Where's my son? Where's my wife?"

"We need to talk with you in a private room," the officer repeated.

"No," I said. "Where's my son and where's my wife? Did my son fall into the pool?"

"Sir," continued the officer, "can we please talk to you privately in this room?"

"Yes, but I need to know now—where are my son and wife? Don't delay the truth here. Tell me now!"

I could feel the gravity of the situation. It was all over the police officer's face and countenance. Talking to me right then must have been one of the toughest things he ever had to do. But I just wanted him to tell me the truth, right then and there.

He explained to me that my son had fallen into the Jacuzzi.

"Did my son die?"

"We think so," said the officer.

It was at that point that I wanted to walk out of the room and go be with my kids. I wanted to go find my wife.

The officer continued. "There a few things you need to know. Your son was transported to the St. Rose Dominican Hospital—the Siena Campus. They tried to resuscitate him, but it didn't work. Your wife is at the hospital with him."

"I've got to get out of here," I said. "I've got to go be with my wife."

"Mr. Cunningham, we have to ask you a few questions."

I could suddenly feel God shifting gears inside my heart, and answering the police officer's questions right then was not what I wanted to do. After I did the best I could, I walked into the next room, grabbed and hugged my children, and began to pray.

"Lord God, you are the giver of life and you're the taker of life. Thank you for my little boy, Christian, you gave us. We are not worthy of him, but we thank you for the two and a half years that you gave to us with him. He was yours first. Thank you for allowing us to have that time with him. He's with you now. We bless you, God. This is no one's fault; this was your divine will. I love you more today than I did yesterday. You know everything and you can do anything. You are sovereign."

I hugged and kissed my family and proceeded out the door to comfort my wife at the hospital.

I was walking at that point, but I know I was being carried just like in the poem "Footprints." My footprints were not the ones in the sand; they were God's. That was the only way I could get through that time—I had to be carried by God.

I got in my car, backed out of the driveway, and began to scream, "Hallelujah! Praise God! Thank you! I love you, God." I refused to display any kind of disrespect, disappointment, or frustration—I refused to do that with God.

The Bible says we're to rejoice in the Lord always, and it repeats *rejoice* (Philippians 4:4). The only way I could get through a tribulation like that was to praise God, as hard as it was in those moments. So very hard.

When I finally reached the hospital, my mind and spirit were flaring in different directions. Friends were there, but I didn't want to talk to anybody. All I wanted to do was see my wife and comfort her.

I approached the counter. "My name's Randall Cunningham. My son just passed away—"

The lady at the counter said, "You have to hold on."

I was not expecting her to say something like that.

I'll be totally honest: anger almost came out of me at that moment. I wanted to say, "My son and wife are in there and you're going to tell me to hold a minute?" But the Bible verse "In your anger do not sin" (Ephesians 4:26) popped into my mind, almost as if God was testing me right then and there.

It's amazing and even a bit frightening where you go on the inside when something of this magnitude happens to you. I was still numb from the initial shock. I wanted to scream. I wanted to cry. I wanted to comfort my kids and my wife. The emotions ran deep and wide, and it was all I could do to keep it together.

A couple of people came up to me and attempted to comfort me, but I wasn't in a let-people-comfort-you mode. I was in a let-me-get-with-my-family mode, for the knife of grief had come upon us and I wanted to comfort my wife before the scar ran too deep.

I was finally led to the room where my wife sat. There she was, holding Christian—our two-and-a-half-year-old angel—in her arms. He had oxygen tubes in his nose. It looked like he was just sleeping. But they told us he was gone. I approached my wife, Felicity, and looked at her.

"Honey, this is no longer our son. Our son is in the arms of the Lord."

She didn't say anything. She just held him.

"We have to let him go," I said. "We have to let him go."

Felicity looked at me. "I don't understand. I laid on him. I did everything the prophets did in the Bible. I prayed over him. I didn't lose faith but prayed that God would bring him back. But he didn't bring him back."

I stared into Felicity's tear-smeared eyes and my heart broke at hearing her words. "Felicity, this is no one's fault, and you will not carry this burden. It belongs to the Lord. It was the Lord's will to take Christian home. This is not your fault; this is no one's fault. It is God's doing."

It was at that point that I knew I had to take my son from his mother's arms because she was not going to let him go. So I took him out of her arms, and when I did, his head fell uncontrollably to the side. Oh, that hurt me deeply to see! That was when I truly realized my son was gone.

I wanted to pull the oxygen cords out of his nose and see him as I remembered him before I had left town. His little body was cold in my arms. The daddy part of me desperately wanted to warm him, but I had to be strong for my wife. She needed me to do what she did not have the strength to do at that moment. I *had* to be strong.

I knew it was God who made me strong in that moment, because no one in the world is strong in a place like that. I was crushed and weak, bolstered up by heavenly hands.

I held him for a few more minutes and then laid hands on him on the bed. There was nothing else we could do. We had to lay him down. No cover, no nothing. Just the lifeless body of my son lying on the hospital bed. I can't describe the feeling in that moment. It was almost as if the only sound in the world I could hear was tears and the only thing I could feel was emptiness. When I laid my son down I was caught in that vacuum of silence and pain.

I grabbed my wife's hand.

We turned and walked out together.

We didn't say a word.

CHAPTER 2

REFLECTION QUESTIONS

Have you ever thanked and praised God during adversity? What made you do that? How hard was it to do? How did it make you feel?

———

How have your life's struggles and pain affected your faith in God? Why?

———

Describe a time when you were aware that God was carrying you, and the only footprints in the sand were his.

———

3

BRACING YOURSELF

DIG DEEP AND HOLD ON

Only people who are capable of loving strongly can
also suffer great sorrow, but this same necessity of loving
serves to counteract their grief and heals them.

—LEO TOLSTOY

Words cannot express the emotion—or lack of emotion—a person feels when faced with tragedy. When Felicity and I returned from the hospital, a few of our pastors and close friends were waiting. Here, as in the hospital, no one said a word. We just sat there, content to be quiet around one another. But I could feel the prayers.

They offered us a meal, but it's difficult to think about food at a time like that. You have no appetite. You feel nothing, but that nothing hurts deeper than you can express. It's an awkward time, I'm sure, for those looking in on the situation. And I've been there before, wishing to comfort someone who's recently lost a loved one. You want to offer food and you want to say something and you want to be there for them. But my wife and I needed to grieve privately. Although we were in the safe confines of God and our closest friends and family, we needed time.

It certainly meant a lot that day to know how deeply people cared. But I just wanted to be in an upstairs room away from it all. Thankfully God kept us near him and away from what we couldn't handle. It was a very emotional time for everyone who knew Christian, a trial for us all to get through individually. God was moving in different directions and in different ways, in all of our hearts. I believe he was doing something supernatural in all of us. He was with us right in the middle of it all. And that was a good thing.

I'm sure that many who were overwhelmed felt left out and may have said to themselves, "Why can't I be a part of the Cunninghams' healing process? I just want them to know that I'm here for them." We felt that too. And we understood why. Christian was as close to an angel as anyone could ever see on this earth. He had that special something that made you tilt your head and ponder, *What is it about this little boy that makes him so lovable?* He was only two and a half, but many people loved him. He was the "church baby," so to speak—all the moms and grandmas doted on him. Teachers at the schools where our older children attended loved him.

Christian was one of thsoe kids who had an intrinsic ability to sense bad things, wickedness. He had that special heightened sense of innocence some people carry with them their whole lives. It was almost like he could sense a person's spirit. If your spirit appeared "heavy," or evil, to him, he wouldn't hang around you. But if you had a good spirit, he would be completely at ease around you. He carried with him a bit of God's grace that would light up a room.

Christian was strong-willed, but not in a bad way. He was an early walker and then, almost the next day it seemed, he was running! On Saturday mornings he knew his older brother, Randall II, had a football game. Christian would wake up and put on his football gear. He had to wear his socks just like the team wore them; he was particular about his uniform. We gave him a pair of pants that was too small for one of the players on Randall II's team.

And when Christian got all decked out in his uniform he looked like the man. If you told him to "make the face" he'd scrunch up his face like he was a real tough football player. He had the football-player persona down pat; he'd run around and then do some push-ups—at age two!

Like all our children, Christian was special to us and to so many others. As a father you never think about the worst thing that could happen to your child. Most of the time you see your children through the rose-colored glasses that I'm showing you right now in describing Christian: they excel at everything they do; they're bound to become great; they walk on clouds. That's what we do as parents. And that's how I saw Christian.

But death and tragedy have a way of revealing the truth of life. In that truth I can see that Christian's greatness was achieved already, at two years old. So God took him. And I was left to lead my family through it.

CARRYING THE WEIGHT

You've probably heard what the Bible says about hardship: "In this world you will have trouble. But take heart! I have overcome the world" (John 16:33). I thank God for his Word! I can also relate to the words of C. S. Lewis in his book *A Grief Observed*:

> We were even promised sufferings. They were part of the programme. We were even told, "Blessed are they that mourn" and I accepted it. I've got nothing that I hadn't bargained for. Of course it is different when the thing happens to oneself, not to others, and in reality, not in imagination.[1]

I can preach all day about getting through life's pains. But on this day, all the rhetoric and theory were blown out the window and I had to carry the weight of this loss on my shoulders. I had to see the hurt and confusion on the faces of my children, my wife, and my aunt. How do you deal with that? What do you say to them and to yourself that will bring any sort of comfort?

A few days after Christian's death, Felicity and I made the decision to have a going-home celebration for our son. Our church sanctuary holds only about six hundred people, and on the day of the ceremony we had to put tents up outside for the overflow of people who showed up to pay their respects.

When I took the stage to celebrate Christian's going to be with the Lord, my mourning was over for the moment. It was time to rejoice in the Lord. In Philippians 4:4 the apostle Paul insists, "Rejoice in the Lord always. I will say it again: Rejoice!" We had shed our tears. We had gone into the darkness of our own souls and searched for answers to the unanswerable. But that sorrow was finished for the moment. It was time to exalt the Most High God for the goodness of two and a half years of our child's life on earth.

Several of my close friends in the music industry came to the memorial service and led those in attendance in a fervent worship time: Israel Houghton, the Katinas, and Deitrick and Damita Haddon. I stood there with my hands raised high and tears streaming down my face, singing from all that was in me.

Here's where I see leadership being important. Did I need to have my time to mourn? Absolutely. But in standing before my family and church in worship and modeling what it looked like to overcome the worst nightmare of a parent, I was leading. There's a worship song by Donnie McClurkin that talks about how, when you've done everything you can to survive and feel you simply can't do any more, all you can do is stand on God's grace. And that's what I was trying to do that morning at that time of celebration. I was standing. Standing on God's principles and strength.

It wasn't just me, however. My wife was standing; my kids were standing. After the time of weeping you must somehow find the ability to take that first step toward healing. Those around us were wondering how we would deal with this. Well, we dealt with it as best we could, and through the constant pain and deep loss, we stood.

I believe that it's in us to stand. Something rises inside us whenever we are backed into a corner. When I looked at my family after those few days of mourning and when I looked out upon my congregation at the memorial ceremony, I realized that we were all still standing and we would continue to fight.

That doesn't mean it's easy. Not a day goes by when I don't think of my beautiful son. And sometimes I want to roll up in a ball and lie on the floor and cry. I miss him *so* much. But I put one foot in front of the other and I start walking and I go on with my day. I continue coaching my track team, the Nevada Gazelles. I continue preparing sermons for Sunday. I continue to love on my family and hang out with friends. I stand because God gives me the strength to do so.

Some days I feel like the biblical character Job. After he had poured out his heart to God, God answered him, saying, "Brace yourself like a man" (Job 38:3). Daily I brace myself. I take courage. I live each day to honor the life of my son. I've found that the more time I spend kneeling, the stronger I can stand.

People will respond to how a leader—a parent, a husband, a pastor—handles adversity. If the leader makes bad decisions in the face of adversity, then he's teaching those who follow him to make bad decisions.

I couldn't afford to do that. Bad decisions with my family during that time would have proved disastrous. My family would have followed me if I had fallen apart and not leaned on my faith during this time.

One of my favorite proverbs instructs, "Trust in the LORD with all your heart and lean not on your own understanding" (Proverbs 3:5). If you want to experience who God is, then you must not only accept him as your Lord, but you must also accept his will for your life. To do that you must trust him and not your own strength.

I've played in high-profile games during my career. I've performed in high-pressure situations, and I've also faced defeat in some of those situations. But nothing in my life could prepare me for the day I came home to find that my son had passed away. In that moment, I suppose, something fired in me—that bit of wiring I've been blessed with where my instincts take over and my emotions stay in check.

On the day that changed my life forever, the only reason I was able to stand at all is because I was taught and mentored to understand that life is not about us. The first chapter of Rick Warren's *The Purpose-Driven Life* begins with, "It's not about you." I understand that truth.

Why is that kind of perspective important? If I view life as revolving around me, then when tragedy hits my entire world will fall apart—because I've constructed a world around me. But if I understand the importance of living for and putting others first, then when tragedy hits I will be able to serve those who need it most. Nothing will have changed; my world will still be intact and I will know exactly how to help.

It's not about Randall. In that moment when I realized I'd lost Christian, I knew I needed to be there for my family.

THE COMING TRIALS

What is a trial? The *New Oxford American Dictionary* defines *trial* as "a formal examination of evidence before a judge, and typically before a jury, in order to decide guilt in a case of criminal or civil proceedings." There are people who *go* on trial, meaning they go into the court system. Sometimes they want to gain an economic upper hand on someone or some business—for money, basically. Sometimes they're on trial for murder.

But *trial* is also defined as "a person, thing, or situation that tests a person's endurance or forbearance." When I look at a trial I see it as a time when God tests us. And when God tests us we, in essence, test him. We test him by holding on to his promises during the trial, seeing if they're real, seeing if we can lean into them. It's within that testing that we develop trust in him.

The poet Lord Byron wrote, "Adversity is the first path to truth." When we are tested in life, the truth of our character—or lack thereof—rises to the surface.

Adversity is the great revealer. We are never more transparent than when life strikes a painful blow. When we are stripped of our pretense and all the fronts we like to put up, we are left with a rather simple choice: either we trust that God will carry us through this thing or we don't.

The way we view adversity also matters. Our culture tends to project trials as negative, whether we're talking about going to trial or we're in a time when bad things are happening to us. But I don't always see trials as negatives. I see them as opportunities. And I understand that the way I view the trials in my life will have a tremendous impact on how I react to those trials.

When we view trials as negative we tend to respond negatively—we get angry or bitter, we allow our pride to swell, and we shake our fist at the sky, yelling, "Why, God? Why are you letting this happen?"

But when we confront trials head-on with a heart full of hope and anticipation, then our reaction to the trial changes. Our first reaction looks less like hand-wringing and more like we're getting ready for the roller-coaster ride. We will experience the ups and downs, but we know in the end it's all for good.

Many of you reading this have heard the adage "To whom much is given, much is required." It's not just an old saying; it's a portion of the Bible that carries significant truth—truth that applies to our lives in very specific ways.

The idea behind the verse is that God gives. He blesses. The more he gives to you, the more he expects from you. I heard this during my time in the NFL, and it was and still is true. When I entered the NFL I had a huge responsibility to my teammates and coaches. Even more, I had a responsibility to my community in New Jersey, where I lived at that time, and to my immediate family and family members spread abroad. All eyes were on me. What was I going to do? That's the reality of playing in the league. You become an instant role model.

Some guys get drafted but then shirk this responsibility. I admit that when I first entered the league I didn't fully understand the enormity of the situation; I didn't immediately seize the opportunity to impact others for good. It's easy to stay self-focused, doing the things that make you feel good or make you more money or make you more popular. This too is a trial. It's a trial to see how you're going to handle yourself. It's a trial to see how you will treat others once you've been given so much.

So trials aren't always negative. Yes, hard times fall upon each of us. Those are the kinds of trials most of us know. But the blessings in life can also serve as trials for us. What will we do with what we've been given?

THANKS FOR THE GOOD AND THE BAD

I've found that in life it's important to appreciate the good times *and* the bad. Easier said than done, true. But if we can do this, we will find great wisdom for the road ahead.

Losing Christian after only two and half years was a trial for me. While my wife, Felicity, and I had him, our lives were rich beyond measure. It was the best of times! Seeing him grow from an infant into a toddler . . . seeing him interact with his older brother, Randall II; and his two older sisters, Vashti and Grace— those were great times! We need to remember, however, that the times of blessing and beauty in our lives are tests as well. Will we live thankful for our blessings? Or will we forget God and the people who helped bless us?

In his poem "Gratefulness," George Herbert asked God for a grateful heart. Not so that he could be thankful to God only when life was good, but so that he could have "such a heart, whose pulse may be thy praise." In other words, he wanted a heart that beat to praise God in all times, good and bad.

This is the kind of thanksgiving we should be living within and modeling to our children and students and peers. It's an ever-present type of thanksgiving, the kind that grows in the good times and flourishes in the deep times of hurt.

The day we lost Christian was one of those deep times. I had to release him to God. Seeing his lifeless body in my wife's arms, and then taking him from my wife and feeling his head limp over my shoulder . . . words cannot explain. The pain I felt in that moment made it difficult to breathe.

I knew the only way we could get through this was to lay him on the hospital bed and walk out. And that's what we did.

We laid him down and walked away from him. It's not like we were leaving him in the nursery at church, able to pick him back up after the service. We were leaving him there for good. Leaving our son with an understanding that God had him in his arms.

I never want anyone to experience that. Even writing about it now I can feel the pressure on my heart, that pressure we experienced when we turned from our little son. Losing your child is not like losing your mother or father. It's not like a grandpa or grandma dying. It's not like a friend passing away—and I've experienced all of these. There's an emotion attached with it that is unexplainable.

The first thing that comes to your mind is "Why?" To shut down that response and instead be able to say, "Thank you, God, for the time we had with him" is a big turn, because our natural response as human beings is to ask why—especially when something happens that is so far outside of normal. It is abnormal to then give thanks. But I'm convinced that is the only way you won't burn up inside with doubt, fear, and frustration.

To people who already struggle with fear and doubt, a tragedy like the one my family experienced might send them over the edge. Hopefully, no matter who you are, when tragedy strikes your first thoughts run to the divine. We all think about God in times of immense trial. But if we already struggle with fear and doubt and something like this happens, then we run the risk of approaching God the wrong way. For me in that moment, when I laid down my son on the bed and walked away, God gave me the strength to choose to say, "Thank you."

I share that with you to show you the lesson I learned about the good and the bad things in life. I've had plenty of success in my life, from playing college football at UNLV to playing for multiple NFL teams and even breaking some passing records along the way. It's easy when things are going well to say, "Thank you, God." But being thankful when your life is grand, though to be expected, is not the measure of your character as a person. Martin Luther King Jr. said, "The ultimate measure of a man is not where he stands in moments of comfort and convenience, but where he stands at times of challenge and controversy."

You will experience trials in your life. They might not be as severe as death, but they can weigh heavily on you. Perhaps you're in the middle of something right now. You may struggle with bracing yourself, with standing strong, with building not only acceptance but a thankful heart in the midst of your situation. But I promise that if you can look to God for your strength, he will be there to bolster you. You will persevere. The end result is ultimately up to God. But you can and will find peace when your attitude is one of faithfulness. And you'll be ready for whatever comes next.

CHAPTER 3
REFLECTION QUESTIONS

We have all faced tragic or difficult situations in our lives. It may be the death of a loved one, or perhaps emotional or physical trauma. If you're able to, detail your own experience here.

━━━

How did you initially respond to this situation? Emotionally? Physically? Verbally? Did you want others around or to be alone? Why?

━━━

How did this experience affect your relationship with God? Did you feel closer to him? Angry? Confused? Thankful? Explain.

━━━

In this situation, were you a leader? If so, how did you handle it? If you were not—if someone else was there leading you through this experience—how did that person help you?

━━━

4

MOVING TOWARD HOPE

CALLED TO SOMETHING MORE

It's about the journey—mine and yours—and the lives we can touch, the legacy we can leave, and the world we can change for the better.

—TONY DUNGY

Some people might remember my initial foray into the NFL. I did not understand patience or contentment then. I was more about me than anyone else. Thankfully, I was fortunate to run into strong men in my career who helped me grow in maturity—off the field. Strength on the field might help you destroy running backs and block and make sacks. But strength off the field will empower you in deeper, more special ways.

Being mentored by these men changed my life forever. They came alongside me, were not afraid to confront me, and were willing to walk beside me—not merely to tell me how to live, but to *show* me how to live. I witnessed firsthand the dynamic influence a mentor can have upon a person. It was this that allowed me to begin my own role as mentor not just with my teammates and congregation but also with my family during our time of grief and renewal.

More than ever we need mentors with whom we can be accountable. I'm convinced that we need men to step up in this department. That is no slight to the need for women mentors. It is, rather, an admission of the ailment from which our country suffers: *fatherlessness*. The building blocks of our culture begin with strong families, and the father is vital to that equation. Children need fathers who are *present*. They need to be taught by their fathers, encouraged by their fathers, loved by their fathers. Mentoring begins with fathers.

As we mature, however, opportunities arise to pour our expertise and wisdom upon the younger generation in general. To do this with honor we need to remember that the mentor is not a master, instructing with harshness. Rather, the mentor's mentality is one of service. Tony Dungy said, "Remember that mentor leadership is all about serving. Jesus said, 'For even the Son of Man came not to be served but to serve others and to give his life as a ransom for many' (Mark 10:45 [NLT])."[1] Tony remains the gold standard when it comes to mentoring. He models the servant's heart well.

BROTHER, GET YOUR LIFE RIGHT

When I first entered the NFL I knew *about* God; after all, I grew up in the church. But it wasn't until I spent time with a guy named Tom Cameron that I realized I didn't really *know* God. Tom and I golfed together one day and afterward he asked, "Randall, are you a Christian?"

"Yeah," I said, "I'm a Christian."

"But are you born again?"

"What? What does that mean?"

As a minister, Tom knew I had no clue what a Christian was.

"Well, Randall, a Christian is a born-again believer—someone in right standing with God. Do you want to become a born-again believer?"

"How long does it take?" I asked.

"It takes as long as saying this prayer with me."

I prayed with Tom, even though I didn't know exactly what it meant. Then I asked him, as the smart aleck I was, "How am I going to know that I've been saved?"

"Oh, now you'll be convicted by the Holy Spirit."

Convicted by the *who*? Holy Spirit?

Enter Reggie White into my life.

Reggie was an intimidating man. Standing six foot five and weighing 325 pounds, he was a giant, even in the NFL. Compare him to one of the top ten defensive ends in the game today, Osi Umenyiora. Osi stands six foot three and weighs 255. The two players most like Reggie in today's game would probably be Julius Peppers and Mario Williams, though neither is close to Reggie's 198 career sacks (yet!).

Not only was Reggie a big man, but he was strong. I used to watch him push offensive linemen out of the way with a one-armed swim move. And if he didn't plow through you or knock you off the ball, he'd outmotor you. He was a relentless player.

His style, mixed with his size and speed, allowed him to collect more sacks than games played while with the Eagles—124 sacks in 121 games.

Reggie was God's tool of conviction. He would get in everybody's face about whatever. He wasn't ever gruff or unkind, but he wasn't afraid to get into your business. His concern for others, however, came from a place of love and leadership. He wanted everybody to go to heaven. And he wanted to win.

Reggie came to the Eagles from the USFL in 1985, the same year the Eagles drafted me. Right away he had no problem confronting me about how I was living and whom I was putting first in my life.

"Randall," he said, "are you a Christian?"

"Yeah, I'm a Christian, Reggie."

"Then, brother, you need to get your life right."

Reggie wasn't blind. He observed my life and how I acted on and off the field. He knew I needed to get right with God. I remember one of the first things he challenged me on was whether or not I paid my tithes to the church.

"No," I said. "I don't pay my tithes to the church. Show me in the Bible where it says that, Reggie." So he did. He opened his Bible to Malachi 3:10: "Bring the whole tithe into the storehouse . . . and see if I will not throw open the floodgates of heaven and pour out so much blessing that there will not be room enough to store it." But Reggie didn't just read the verse; he read the whole chapter to me. As he read I sat there thinking, *Man, I'm making about three hundred thousand dollars a year, and this brother's telling me I have to give 10 percent to the church?*

I knew he was right.

So the next Sunday I went to church and wrote a check for one hundred thousand dollars. The next day I received a check for five hundred thousand dollars. It was part of my bonus money from that season. Was the storehouse opening up before my eyes? In that instant I knew that God was real and that he would do what he said he'd do. He proved to me in that moment that he would "throw open the floodgates of heaven," just as the verse in Malachi said. God knew in advance what I would do, and he had provided for my faithfulness in advance.

I determined at that point that on December 31 of every year I would pay my tithe. And God set it up that for four straight years I received a half-million-dollar bonus check on the first of every year. God repeatedly proved to me that if I showed myself to be faithful in my giving, he would throw open the floodgates.

That's how Reggie White mentored me. He made himself part of my life. He was faithful to his convictions and allowed those convictions to penetrate into the way I was living. He challenged me and encouraged me to make my faith something that was *real* and *powerful* in the lives of other players.

Reggie also challenged me to get involved in Bible study—which I did. The next thing I knew, Cedric Brown, one of my teammates, was leading Bible studies at my house. It seemed all the lessons I heard him give were about my life. One study was in the book of Romans and centered on authority. At that time I was dealing with rebellion. I thought, *Is he writing each of these sermons for me?* It seemed like God was talking directly to me through his Word.

Reggie's and Cedric's influence on me began a new chapter in my life. It was a spiritual awakening through and through that had actually begun back on the day of the 1985 NFL draft. On that day, as I walked up to the podium where the NFL commissioner had announced that the Eagles had made me the first quarterback selected in the draft, I remember saying, "God, I must owe you something."

Yes, he replied. *You owe me your life.*

That little prayer exchange was as clear as day to me. God's words stuck in my heart. And as I slowly began to clean up my life, Reggie and Cedric found their way into the process. Others followed—pastor Troy Johnson, John Michaels (who became my pastor), and Keith Johnson (who was chaplain for the Minnesota Vikings). I was fortunate to have these strong men of character and faith in my life. I credit them for showing me how to stand for what's right when it's so easy not to.

But I also credit them for instilling within me a hunger and thirst to deepen my faith, through Bible study and a prayer life. Troy Johnson especially played a major role in helping me understand how to pray and to recognize my spiritual gifts. It's easy to waltz into the NFL and feel like you own the world and you know everything. Teams pay you a king's ransom to play a game you love, and it seems like you can grab everything the world offers. But if a player enters the league without a true understanding of who he is, he will struggle on a personal level—be it with money or women or fame.

As my personal faith grew, I began to see just how deeply I was affected by the example of these other men and the power of God in my life. I watched God bless me by bringing my wife, Felicity, into my life. Through my relationship with her, God began teaching me—and continues to teach me—what it means to love someone unconditionally. That love lesson strengthens not only my marriage but also my character, and it helps me love others the way God does.

Through my faith in God I found a depth of love that allowed me to love others without condition. That was a major epiphany for me. I was even able, through God's strength, to love people who hurt me. Felicity and I were able to love people even when they wronged us, without expecting anything from them in return.

These aspects of life transformed me but did not come *from* me; they came *to* me. They were part of my spiritual deepening as I was mentored and challenged by men who really cared for me.

DEVELOP REVERENCE

When I think about the change that occurred in my life, from the time I met Reggie until now, I can characterize it with the word *reverence*. Our culture tends to celebrate the irreverent. We care only to revere ourselves. But that kind of twisted self-love leads to selfishness, greed, self-worship, and debilitating pride.

Understanding reverence was a major shift for me. When I developed a serious reverence for God, when I put others' needs before my own, I was able to handle the good *and* bad situations of my life and career with grace. Here's how that reverence can save a person.

Reverence Leads to Joy

First, reverence can give us joy. By *joy* I don't mean a temporal happiness. Some people say that happiness comes from within. I think that's true to a point. But most people see happiness as a state of being—we're happy because our life circumstances dictate it. We get a raise; we're happy. We receive the birthday gift we were hoping for; we're happy.

It's interesting to me that America's Founding Fathers thought it good to include "the pursuit of happiness" in the Declaration of Independence. I think we may misunderstand what exactly they were getting at with that reference—we twist it to be all about getting what we can. But it's not about that. Philosopher Mortimer Adler said that the happiness they speak of in that great document is not a state of being that we ever achieve. Rather, it is the state of being we find ourselves in when our life is nearly over. Only when we face death can we survey our life and say, "I've achieved happiness."

Happiness, in this regard, equals the sum total of our entire life. It reflects the good things we've done—how we've served others and the memories we've made. This kind of happiness is different from the shallow, self-centered word we toss around on a daily basis. Yet it is still not akin to joy. Joy is something far deeper.

Joy connects to my faith. Whereas happiness gives me feeling, joy gives me strength. Happiness tends to come in the good times. But joy is something that will rise in whatever time, in whatever life throws at me. Joy is something that comes from my core being. Joy reflects who I am in God—that's the reservoir I draw from.

I once heard a preacher say, "Jesus is out for bigger game than your happiness; he's working on your holiness. Faith is not learned, as we would like, at a spiritual retreat or even in a sermon; it's only learned in the fiery furnace of trial and hardship."[2] I think part of the "bigger game" that Jesus is after is the joy connected to our faith. It's a joy made perfect through the fires of trials, a joy that looks beyond temporal feelings and into the beyond of God's love for us.

I was very *happy* to attend Randall II's T-ball games when he was a little kid. But the *joy* of the Lord came over me whenever I saw him hit the ball and run around the field—when I saw his face light up with something that came from deep within him. That light was joy. And it did something inside of me. I was thankful that I had a son. I was thankful to God for blessing him with the ability to play sports.

My gratitude to God gives me the expression of joy. When I have joy I have a hope that happiness cannot give. Since joy comes from God, then joy contains the promise of what my life holds. And it's my sense of reverence for God that allows me to experience it.

If God holds my life, what can hurt me? If God is the source of my joy, then what obstacle can I not overcome?

Reverence Leads to Perseverance

People want to read positive, happy stories with a neat life lesson tied up in a bow. I get that. But let's not overlook the *benefit* of life pain.

You and I will endure a certain amount of pain. Our experiences will be different, but we will be able to relate to one another on some level. Whether you lose your mother or your child, whether you lose your job or discover that your spouse has been unfaithful, you will feel the sting that accompanies life. You choose how you will respond to that sting. You can choose to reflect on it with thankfulness, or you can choose to be lost in an ocean of bitterness. The key is to view pain not as a deterrent but as a stepping-stone to greater things. As Charlie "Tremendous" Jones said, "Things don't go wrong and break your heart so you can become bitter and give up. They happen to break you down and build you up so you can be all that you were intended to be."

In the introduction to this book I talked about that specific time in your life when you will have to make a decision. You will need to decide how to respond to the pain. The writer and poet Maya Angelou said, "You may not control all the events that happen to you, but you can decide not to be reduced by them." You must decide: Will the hurt and obstacles in life keep you down and define you? Or will you receive what life dishes out to you and turn it into a learning experience?

The biggest contributing factor to your decision will be your interpretation of and response to the pain you feel. Will you interpret your life pain as a deep wound that you carry around? Or will you interpret it as an opportunity to allow life's greatest blows to help you grow? I promise you: if you allow your reverence for God's work in your life to be the foundation of your expectations and response, you will choose the latter.

When I stood in the hospital room with my wife, holding Christian's lifeless body in my arms, I had no choice but to lay him down. But even though I laid him down physically, I could have held on to him on the inside. I could have clung to him on the drive home and the next morning at breakfast.

In truth, this is exactly what the grieving process is all about: your time to hold on to the pain, the grief, and the hurt just a bit longer. For me, the grieving process was the *mental activity* of laying Christian down. If I had continued to hold on to him—through the dark valley of regret, for example—then I would not have been able to move on from that moment. The memory and the anguish would have haunted me. My work in the church, my relationship with my wife and children, my work in the community—all of these would have been affected in a deep way. I would have been carrying Christian around with me, believing that I was unable to lay him down.

Live at all and you will feel pain. Pain, in fact, is not the issue. The issue you must confront is what to do with the scar that comes after the initial sting of the hit.

In football, when I received a hard hit I'd wince but continue with the game—playing hurt if need be. I never looked at a defensive end after he hit me and asked him why he hit me so hard. I found a way to play through the ringing in my head or the throbbing in my leg or the stinging sensation going up my arm.

But sometimes, hard hits cause injuries. Those injuries often leave scars from surgery—like the one on my knee! I had to rehabilitate my knee. It took time and was painful. But if I had done nothing, I'd still be limping around and would never have played again.

You may be living your days carrying pain on the inside. Maybe you can barely get through your day without crying or feeling overwhelmed.

But there's another way. You can renew your perspective and refuse to view the pain in your life as an anchor weighing you down. Rather, you can develop a reverence that views pain as the beginning of the healing process—as the catalyst that sets your course to becoming a better person.

Michael Jordan knew a thing or two about overcoming obstacles and hardship. In July 1993, his father was murdered at a highway rest area by two teenagers. Not long after, Jordan surprised the world with his early retirement from professional basketball. But after a brief respite from the game, no doubt dealing with the grief from losing his father, Jordan returned to the NBA and won three more championships with the Chicago Bulls. "Obstacles don't have to stop you," Michael said. "If you run into a wall, don't turn around and give up. Figure out how to climb it, go through it, or work around it."

USE OBSTACLES FOR TRAINING

I love coaching track. I coach a club team comprised of some of the best high school track athletes in the Las Vegas area.

As their coach I work very hard to push and teach them to be the best ever—to be excellent in their preparation and to overcome the mental obstacles that weigh them down as they compete.

As the rest of these chapters unfold, I'd like you to pretend that you've joined my track team and that I'm your coach, coming alongside you as you prepare for a meet. (Yes, you can pretend you're seventeen again if that will make it fun for you!)

The difference is we're not talking about the high hurdles. You and I are talking about whatever it is that's inside you keeping you from being the complete person God created you to be.

We're going to use whatever obstacles hinder you and turn the situation around, making it something that fuels your ability to lay down whatever it is that ails your spirit, whatever it is that breaks your heart on a daily basis, whatever it is that keeps you locked up and away from those who love you the most.

But to accomplish this you must suspend the need to hold on to your pain. You must look at the obstacle, the splinter in your soul, and have the courage to embrace it, lay it down, and move on with your life.

CHAPTER 4
REFLECTION QUESTIONS

*Have you ever had a mentor in your life? Write down
the details of this person—where you met him or her and
how the mentoring relationship came into being.*

———

*How did this person mentor and guide you? Was it personally?
Spiritually? In the business world? At school? Explain.*

———

*If you had a mentor, what are some of the key lessons your mentor
taught you? Were you open to them? How have they affected your
life since learning them? Have you continued to follow them?*

———

*Have you ever mentored someone else? If so, how did this
mentoring relationship come into being? Are you still mentoring?*

———

*What are the key lessons you gave that person? Why did you feel
they were important? Did they effect positive change in your pupil?*

———

*Are there any lessons you wish your mentor had
taught you? Any lessons you wish you'd given
your own pupil? What are they and why?*

———

*If you have not been someone's mentor yet, do you think you
would be willing to be one at this point in your life? Explain.*

———

PRINCIPLE 1
FRICTION IS YOUR FRIEND

WHY OBSTACLES ARE GOOD TRAINING

It's hard to beat a person who never gives up.

—BABE RUTH

For Christmas 2011 my wife asked me what I wanted. I told her I wanted a stationary bike. Is that a strange thing to ask for when you're forty-eight? Shouldn't I have asked for a sports car or something like that? Well, I had my reasons. One being to stay in shape! Despite what people may think, life after the NFL is life like everyone experiences it. If you don't use it, you'll certainly lose it.

During my football career I used to perform interval training on a stationary bike. Interval training, for those unfamiliar with the term, is when you alternate between sprinting and a slow pedal cadence on the bike. So, for example, I'd sprint for a set amount of time—trying to get my RPMs up to a predetermined level—and then I'd back it off.

I loved this kind of training because it would strengthen not only my legs but also my mental toughness. The longer I rode, the more I'd increase the resistance. The tougher the resistance, the more my legs would burn, which would make me work that much harder to finish the workout.

In both working out and playing sports, there's always a point at which you want to give up physically. It's at that point where your training kicks in—and not just your physical training. Your mental training is the key element that will help you get past the burn and into the fourth quarter.

Finally I had my bike and could start training again. But there was another reason I wanted the equipment. I wanted to train my track team on it, as well as my own children, who are all involved in sports at some level. I wanted to show them how to do interval training. Football or track, it doesn't matter; you're going to get tired. I wanted my young athletes to be able to train through the burn that comes when you're tired.

I would get them each of the atheletes on the bike and begin at level one. Then we'd move up levels of difficulty, from one up to three, then to five, seven, nine, eleven, and so on. Once they reached level nine, that's when the "race" would really begin. The earlier levels weren't really that difficult and served more as a warm-up. By the time they reached level nine, they were getting stronger.

I've continued this practice since then. And it's made a difference in my team. Now, if one of my hurdlers is starting to get caught from behind, he has the strength to go even farther because he is stronger. He's built a strength that goes beyond what is demanded in the average race. When the battle comes within the race, he has a well to tap into and run harder, to be stronger!

What's great to see on my track team is that they run *away* from people near the end of a race. When the other runners begin to tire, our team digs in and either pulls away to victory or catches other runners. The whole team has qualified for the AAU Junior Olympics and the USATF Junior Olympics.

FAT OR FRICTION

When I stop and think about that stationary bike and how important it has been for my own development as a player and now as a coach, I can't help but think about the work it takes to become strong. When I say "work," I mean the tension and resistance it takes to build muscle along with mental toughness.

It's impossible to wake up one day and suddenly become strong. You can't drink protein shakes and expect to get stronger or bigger without actually working out. It takes hard labor. Regardless of all the commercials on television and the diet books with different steps, you simply cannot lose weight and keep it off by starving yourself. If you remain inactive you will put the weight back on in a hurry—and likely not really lose much weight to begin with. You must put in the work to lose weight and become physically fit.

I've heard it said that advertising and marketing gurus encourage Internet users to buy products by making the pathway to purchasing easy. They say a website needs to create an online presence that has very little resistance, or *friction*. What they mean is that you don't want there to be several steps before a user can make a purchase; you want the process as streamlined as possible.

I can see the value in that. I love the ease that comes with buying online. Make it tough and I'm frustrated. Make it happen in one click, like Amazon's "Buy now with 1-Click" option, and I'm in.

But I'm not talking about Internet shopping. I'm talking about what it takes to build strength to overcome in order to overcome the other runners so that you can attain the prize. You want friction. You need friction in order to build up muscle and stamina. If you don't exercise your muscles on a regular basis, you won't grow stronger, and when the race gets tough in the last hundred yards your opponents will overcome you.

Likewise, in football, if you haven't done the work in the off-season and in training camp to make yourself stronger and better, an athlete who *has* put in the work will eclipse you. An NFL team program is a good example of what it takes to build physical and mental muscle. Once on the team you begin the rigor of the OTAs (optional training activities) and then the mandatory off-season workouts, culminating in training camp—several weeks of conditioning, drills, meetings, study, and weight lifting.

These training exercises keep players mentally sharp as well as sharp on the fundamentals of their positions. The repetition of these training exercises is paramount. ESPN commentators and former NFL coaches talk often about the "reps" of a player. If you receive first-team reps, then you're getting the bulk of the reps in practice. Some may not think that's all that important, but it is. Working over and over with the same people helps develop continuity in play as well as like-mindedness in the mental aspect of the game.

If you want to build physical and mental muscle, then you need to put in the work it takes to become a better player. That work involves constant friction: friction in weight training, friction in conditioning, friction with coaches in the meeting room. You must tear down muscle to build it. You must stretch yourself physically in order to become stronger and faster.

Increasingly, I see young athletes expecting to *be* great without putting in the time and sacrifice to *become* great. I think our culture of entitlement contributes to this thinking, as well as the media, which depicts winning championships and getting drafted but fails to show the enormous daily sacrifice and commitment it takes to achieve that type of success.

During the 2012 Summer Olympic Games in London, Nike ran a commercial about *greatness*. The commercial depicts an overweight preteen boy wearing a baggy white shirt running toward the camera. At first he is a long way off, so all you see is the horizon and an open road. He's not running fast—just a slow, steady pace. He's sweating and looking past the camera, determined and focused. All you hear are his feet moving over the road. The boy is in the middle of nowhere with no one watching—open fields on either side of the road.

The voice-over says that we tend to think that greatness is something "reserved for a chosen few—for prodigies, for superstars." But in reality, we are *all* capable of greatness.

Greatness, according to this commercial, is something anyone can achieve as long as you are willing to endure the toil and lonely times of hard work when no one is watching. It doesn't matter what kind of person you've been up to that point; it only matters that you put one foot in front of the other and endeavor to take on the process of building greatness. I like how this commercial inspires greatness without shying away from the friction and pain it takes to achieve it. We can all achieve greatness, yet few do. It comes down to us and the decisions we make.

This is part of the human condition really: beauty can come from ashes, pain can provide the opportunity for greatness, and anything worth doing will require something of you—something valuable.

Our lives run on friction; greatness is born of it.

KEEPING IT REAL

I remember clearly one specific game that I played against the Eagles' divisional rival, the Washington Redskins. It was a scorching hot day with 100 percent humidity. You know the type of day—you can't walk to your mailbox without sweating through your shirt.

The night before the game it poured rain. All I was thinking about was how sloppy the field was going to be for the game. The next morning, however, when we arrived at the stadium we found out that the grounds crew had covered the field.

That was good. But we couldn't do anything about the humidity.

Now remember, I'm a Vegas guy. I'm used to the heat. But I'm used to *dry* heat! Don't get me wrong—dry Vegas heat is still brutal, and 108 degrees is 108 degrees. But on the East Coast, 100 degrees feels like you're living in a boiling soup bowl. It was that kind of a day!

I wasn't accustomed to the air sticking to me like a blanket. The moment I walked onto the field I was dripping with sweat. It was awful. Sweat saturated my jersey and my pants. It felt like sweat was saturating my pads, making my whole uniform heavier.

But I was determined not to let humidity hamper my play. I took the field in the first half and poured myself into every aspect of the game—I was dialed in, calling plays from the huddle and doing my best to execute the plays and lead my teammates.

By the time we jogged into the locker room for halftime, I was done. I wanted to fold up camp—I felt as though I had nothing left in me. You know the feeling: you've been in a zone and pouring yourself into a task and then you hit the wall.

Well, I had hit the wall. And not only me but our entire team.

All I could think about was how much I wanted to sit down and eat everything in sight and guzzle a gallon of water. I needed to get some kind of sustenance in me, and fast. Usually at halftime they give you a bag of oranges to eat. As soon as I reached the locker room I ate every orange I could find! I might have even eaten the peels, I was *that* hungry!

I had a whole second half to endure.

We reached the fourth quarter. I don't even remember who the opposing quarterback was at this point, but we were going back and forth all game and found our teams tied up near the end of the game.

At that point I was thinking, *I have nothing left to give*. I had taken a few hard hits and had experienced double vision. I think I had a concussion. My thoughts focused on just getting through one play at a time.

As exhausted and beat up as I was, though, I wanted to keep going. Buddy Ryan was our coach at the time, and he was the kind of coach you wanted to play for—you wanted to give your all for him on every play. I didn't want to let him down. I didn't want to let my teammates down. They needed strong leadership at that time in the game. I had to keep going.

I stepped into the huddle and, panting, started calling the play.

"Split right; hot right; eighty-three!"

I had to take a deep breath to continue.

"On . . . one. On . . . one. Ready, break!"

We approached the line of scrimmage, which felt like a mile from the huddle. Just squatting down in my stance was tough work! But we executed the play and headed back to the huddle to call another play.

As we formed our huddle I could see the Redskins players, and they weren't huddling up. They were all kneeling down in their positions; they didn't even huddle to call the defense. They were panting worse than we were.

"Look!" I yelled to my guys. "They're tired too! Buddy Ryan runs us hard. We're in better shape than they are! Come on, guys! Let's go!"

It was like something snapped in the ten guys staring back at me. My words took us to another level, giving us confidence and vision for the task at hand. I'd reminded my teammates of how we'd trained endlessly for such a moment as this, honing our skills and our stamina. We were prepared.

Dropping back and firing the ball as hard as I could, I threw the game-winning pass to Keith Jackson. I don't know how he caught it. I guess he wanted the game to end as much as I did that day. Keith jumped for it, snatched it out of the air, and brought both feet inbounds.

I went crazy! He went crazy! We all went crazy! The fans went crazy! I was running around the field yelling, celebrating with my teammates. Keith tried to spike the ball but it slipped out of his hand—it looked ugly. But we didn't care. We laughed and celebrated.

From where or from whom did we receive energy? In one way I guess that's obvious: *God*. But our win also came from an unflinching approach to friction in our training. We won because we were ready, because we'd prepared, we had endured. At a time when we felt like we couldn't go any further, we'd tapped into our strength and taken it to victory.

Friction fills life. It's everywhere. I'm writing this chapter on a Monday. Every Monday millions of us trudge through the friction of our jobs, the friction of our family relationships, and the ever-present friction of our inner selves. We rub against one another in the way we treat each other, and we rub against the seemingly immovable reality of our occupations. The dynamics at the office or on the work site, the dynamics of friends or family members loving us and betraying us—each day holds its own bit of friction.

The way we perceive this friction propels us toward success and prosperity. Or it weighs on us, anchoring us to a lifestyle of exasperation and negativity. Which will it be for you?

I can sit here all day writing inspirational stories of athletes who have committed themselves to making their bodies the best they can be. But the real point of all this is your desire to embrace friction and change your perspective on the trials life throws at you. Will you view them with disdain, as something to be avoided? Or will you view them as part of your life process—building you mentally and spiritually, readying you for anything that comes your way?

If you choose the latter, you'll find the mental and spiritual strength to power you through the hard times in life.

How? The answer to that question is not a magic mantra, a shortcut, or an easy pill to swallow. The answer lies in old-fashioned perseverance.

CHAPTER 5
REFLECTION QUESTIONS

*Detail a time when you experienced friction
in your personal or business life.*

———

*How did you handle that situation? Were you able
to use the friction in a positive way? Explain.*

———

*Now detail a time in your spiritual life when you
experienced friction or a crisis of faith.*

———

*How did you handle your spiritual friction? Do you
feel stronger for experiencing it? Or did you struggle
with your faith? Are you still struggling?*

———

*Think again about the time in your life when you
experienced the most friction—mental, spiritual, or other.
Are you thankful in the end that you went through it? Or
do you wish it had never happened? Why or why not?*

———

6

PRINCIPLE 2
DOWN AT HALFTIME

PERSEVERANCE IN THE TOUGH TIMES

Never give in—never, never, never, in nothing great or small, large or petty, never give in except to convictions of honour and good sense. Never yield to force; never yield to the apparently overwhelming might of the enemy.

—WINSTON CHURCHILL

What happens when you need to power through something? As a quarterback, I would often face a defense coming at me with rushes that our team wasn't as prepared for as we thought we were. Likewise, in other areas of life, oftentimes we're met with a stubborn obstacle that seems to require more from us than we think we are capable of. It's not like you can hop on a stationary bike right in the middle of the obstacle and build your perseverance muscles. But there are things you can do that will help you persevere. We just need to remind ourselves to do them.

Let's say you're going through some friction at work. Day in and day out you're putting up with the same person who doesn't like you. How do you respond?

Or perhaps you're putting in time at work, but in the back of your mind you think you're not getting paid enough. How can you motivate yourself to keep going?

Maybe you're going through a difficult time in your marriage or perhaps you're having a frustrating time at home with one of your children acting out—needing discipline yet trying your patience.

In all these scenarios your mental toughness as a coworker or parent or spouse needs to be stronger than the circumstance. You have to be tough because mental weakness in any of these scenarios will hamper you and pull you down.

When you're mentally weak you end up caving in to your emotions and responding out of those emotions. In your anger you lash out at your spouse and begin talking about separation. In your frustration you raise your voice at your kids when they misbehave. In your impatience you manipulate the irritating coworker and then fall to their level.

But if you persevere and stay mentally tough in these scenarios, you end up working things out with your spouse, not berating them or letting anger control you—refusing to give up just because you're going through a rough patch. You end up being the one who receives the big promotion while the annoying coworker moves on to agitate someone else.

Our culture is one of instant gratification. If things go wrong at work, we get another job. If we struggle in our marriage, we get another spouse. This is sad. Have we become so soft as a culture, so "me-centered," that we can't see the value of perseverance?

There is a reward to developing mental toughness. And that reward is won through the trials of life that, through friction, bring us mental and spiritual strength. If we develop a high tolerance level, if we can get stronger when we hit level nine and not falter, then we can withstand anything the world throws at us.

POWER DOWN TO BUILD UP

There are definitely some practical things you can do when facing a trial.

Let's say you're arguing with a family member. This may seem trivial to you, but this scenario is something every person encounters, sometimes on a daily or weekly basis. So let's break it down. What can you do to defuse this trial?

Shut Up

Don't badger the other person and don't exacerbate the situation with more arguing. Think clearly for a moment and ask permission to be excused from the discussion if need be. If you're struggling through a long-term argument that seems to get worse every time you or the person you're arguing with brings up the topic, this still applies. Too often we underestimate the importance of being quiet and letting time heal the situation. More often than not, we should allow things to work themselves out at their own pace, without our needing to argue them to death.

Take a Breath

Go for a walk. Hit the nearest park and cruise the pathways, taking in the beauty of creation around you. Or if you're a person who likes to shoot baskets, do that. If you like to jog, then jog. It's amazing how time calms us and quells the wrath inside us— keeping it from oozing all over our relationships. Oftentimes, getting away from a stressful situation and focusing on something more relaxing can be therapeutic and allow you to realize that things aren't as traumatic as you initially believed.

Be Thankful

As you walk and adore the beauty of creation, spend some time thanking God for the things he has given you: your life, your family, your friends, a house, a car—all good and perfect gifts in this life, and all bestowed by our heavenly Father above (James 1:17). Take a moment to acknowledge that. When we spend more time being thankful for all the blessings in our life, the obstacles in our life begin to feel smaller.

Get Some Perspective

When we actually take a moment to think about the situation and about our actions and words, we see things more clearly. If we are too close to something, our view is limited and we can see only a portion of it. But if we step back and take a look at the whole situation from afar, we can see all around it and take in the big picture. Like climbing to a mountaintop to see the way ahead, take the time to see the situation from a different perspective.

When life gets ugly you should always take a moment and look to your safety outlets. Don't have any? Well, then spend some time discovering what you like to do—that activity that will take your mind off the stress at hand and give you a bit of peace—and do it. The key is to do whatever it takes to gain perspective.

If you don't like to go to the park, then go shopping. Window-shopping can be the beginning. You don't have to spend money and create another issue with your spouse.

Or sit down in a quiet place and read your Bible or listen to your favorite worship songs. Tell God you love him. Find that special thing that will help you regain your perspective on life and the situation at hand and discipline yourself to do it when times get tense.

It may feel odd at first and seem too much outside your daily routine, but that's the point. I want to encourage you to insert these breathing moments into your routine. Don't let things build up until finally you break down. You'll be surprised how beneficial a brisk walk in the park can be to a tired mind and stressed spirit. These breathing moments will help you develop perseverance by giving you the margin to handle tough situations.

Like you, I need those breathing moments. I do my best to allow myself to take a mental break on a daily basis. I often find myself facing stressful situations. Being a pastor carries with it a certain weight, and if I'm not careful I can become overly stressed. Being a father is also stressful and carries an immense responsibility. So I have to have an outlet on a daily basis to keep everything straight.

Once I asked my pastor, "Pastor John, what do you do when you feel like things are crashing down on you?"

"Randall," he said, "I go to my out-of-state cabin in Utah and just relax. But that's me. We all need to have an outlet, something that will help us regain our strength and perspective."

Well, I'm not a cabin guy, but I *am* a movie guy. I like to go watch a matinee. I have no problem paying a few bucks for a chance to sit in a cool, relaxing place. I say "watch," but the funny thing is I fall asleep every time! I don't watch the movie; the movie watches me! You may think I'm crazy, but that therapy works for me. It's amazing how refreshed and centered I feel when I do that. I feel like a laptop whose battery has been drained and then gets plugged into the wall for a few hours. In the Disney movie *WALL-E*, the little robot wakes up in the morning all run down, then he opens his solar panels and powers back up. That's how I feel when I leave the theater: totally rejuvenated!

If I don't get to a matinee, then I'll take a drive and look at real estate—and there's a lot of it for sale in the Vegas area. I don't intend to buy; I just like to browse. I enjoy being in my truck and cruising around town appreciating the beautiful homes that man has been able to construct because of the mind God has given him. I appreciate good craftsmanship, like the stone front on a house. It allows me to relax and refresh.

When I retired from the NFL the first time, I *really* needed an outlet. I was so frustrated with life in 1996 that I just needed to unplug from it all. I was at a place in my mind and heart where I hated football and I didn't want to be around a lot of people. I just wanted to ride off into the sunset and go golfing every day.

Okay, that's a myth. Retirement is not about playing golf every day. It's about getting into a life rhythm after your career ends. What was going to be my new rhythm?

As I mentioned before, I started a marble and granite company. I know most people during that time of my life were scratching their heads wondering why I was quitting the NFL to start a granite company. But the truth is, I enjoyed watching a stone that had no shine or shape to it become something beautiful. My company installed custom granite and marble kitchen countertops. We also did some marble flooring. I loved going into a home and refurbishing it. I can't begin to explain how this enterprise renewed me. It helped me deal with all the pressures of the world that I felt I was carrying on my back.

I'd go into the shop and get a five-hundred-pound slab of black granite. I'd do all the measurements and then cut it with a diamond saw that would slice right through it perfectly. I'd glue the pieces together, and then we'd polish the stone and grind it down and sand it and wet-polish it—we'd go through grades and grades of sandpaper doing whatever we needed to do to get that piece of stone into a countertop. Finally, we'd deliver and install it.

What joy! I loved leaving a home after installing a countertop. I loved the sense of accomplishment at the beauty we left behind. And when I'd clean up the shop and reflect on all we'd done in that day, it brought enormous satisfaction.

Maybe you like to work with your hands or perhaps you're an arts-and-crafts type of person. I can tell you from experience that digging into work like that will give you a sound mind as well as push you physically. For me, it was a release *and* a retreat—a chance to take a breath after playing quarterback in the NFL and to gain perspective.

You must have some kind of outlet in life—something that keeps you sane and healthy. You need something that keeps you calm, focuses your mind and heart on something that brings you joy, and renews your body and soul.

What's your outlet?

Take a break from reading and, if you have a journal or use a web-based note-taking app, define your outlets. Go a step further and schedule your outlets. For some people if they don't mark their calendar with an event or task, it will never get accomplished. So schedule your daily walk, run, nap, or cruise around town. Set up an alert on your phone; get that breathing time showing up in your in-box.

YOU ARE MIND, BODY, AND SOUL

If you don't understand how to find peace in your life, like my time working with stone, then the trials—the *friction*—will win. Not only will the friction win, it will beat you down. There are new studies now showing a small but consistent link between high and regular levels of stress and heart disease. Heart disease is the number-one killer of men and women in America. There's even evidence indicating that stress can actually affect how your blood clots.

If you search medical websites you'll find plenty of articles detailing what a stressful lifestyle looks like and how to cope with it. Maintaining high levels of stress affects your sleeping habits and your blood pressure; it can even cause psychological problems.

Winning the friction race is all about how you cope and the position you put yourself in. But if you look at the trials in life that will either build perseverance or turn you into a stress ball, you'll find a truth I like to call *wholeness*.

How is wholeness a truth? Well, I believe that each person is made in the image of God. I believe that God formed man out of the earth and breathed life into him. Interesting to think that we have the breath of God in our lungs, isn't it? But I believe we do. I also believe God not only gave us a physical body but endowed each person with a soul. It has been said that a person *has* a body but *is* a soul. I think that's correct.

We are composite beings. And what I mean by that is that we are made up of more than just one part; we are made of many parts: a mind, a body, and a soul. These parts, I believe, are related as well—intertwined. How we physically handle the daily tension of life, as well as the larger tragedies of life, correlates directly to how we handle it spiritually.

Too often we think we can overeat without it having an effect on how we deal with things mentally or spiritually. We get stressed, so we eat. And eat. And eat. And eat.

But overeating can lead to obesity, which then leads to inactivity or loafing. When you lead an inactive life you run the risk of falling into depression or becoming negative. You can become self-conscious about your weight and develop a cynical disposition. Obesity can also lead to serious health issues like diabetes and heart disease.

Likewise, if one drink after work turns into three or four, you run the risk of alcoholism or making poor moral judgments, not to mention endangering folks if you get behind the wheel. I personally don't drink and I don't judge those who choose to, but the negative effects associated with alcohol cannot be denied.

These are just two examples of how the way some people deal with stress can lead to unhealthy living both physically and spiritually.

The great theologian J. I. Packer once wrote that we, as human beings, were meant to run on "soulish" things—things like worship and service and honesty and self-discipline. This is how we bear God's moral image.

What happens when you don't nourish those soulish things in your life? You begin making bad decisions at work. Your moral guard goes down and you might fall prey to pornography or an affair. You begin to speak sharply to your wife and children—and if that becomes a pattern you then run the risk of rearing children who dishonor you because they don't respect you. In short, you end up distancing yourself from God and those closest to you.

I know some people who brush off the notion that they need to cultivate the soulish part of who they are, thinking that at some point down the line they'll take care of it. But down the line is always too late. If we don't make the decision to stay balanced in body, mind, and soul today, then when tragedy hits, we will feel lost and overwhelmed.

However, when we allow our bodies and our minds and our souls the opportunity to rejuvenate, when we take some time off during seasons of stress and friction, then we allow our whole being to heal and grow stronger.

That's why I believe each person needs some kind of outlet each day for the soul. Even if you take just a few minutes in the morning for prayer and devotions, you are setting your mind on the right track from the get-go. We are hardwired to take a break. I tell people, "That's why God created vacations—so you can rest and get re-centered."

Did God really create vacations? Of course. He was the first vacationer!

Remember the Sabbath

When God created the world he took the seventh day off. He took a vacation from all his work. Moses wrote, "In six days the LORD made the heavens and the earth, and on the seventh day he rested and was refreshed" (Exodus 31:17).

God doesn't need to take a break. He's God! But when he rested on the seventh day he created for us a model by which we should live our lives. Do your work. Drive yourself to excellence.

But take a day off at the end of the week and play with your kids or your siblings or go out with friends. Spend time at church and sing. Go to a football game and laugh and cheer. Take a nap.

When we take a day off or head out for a vacation, we are maintaining our "soulish" existence. We achieve a life balance that so many in our world fail to do. Too often we push and push until we break physically and mentally. That has become the norm for us. But should it be?

This leads me to another point about cultivating our soulishness as we take care of the physical needs in life: *wisdom*.

Cultivate Wisdom

In our society wisdom is often thrown to the curb. That's unfortunate because wisdom can save us from a ton of grief. I love this verse in the book of Ephesians: "Be very careful, then, how you live—not as unwise but as wise, making the most of every opportunity, because the days are evil. Therefore do not be foolish, but understand what the Lord's will is" (5:15–17).

Paul, the writer of these verses, is cautioning a church congregation—people like you and me—to be wise in the way they were living.

Look at the verses and notice what Paul is *not* saying: he's not saying don't ever take a risk in life or don't ever try anything that looks like it's beyond you. No, he says make the most of the opportunities you're afforded in this life. Yes, he leads with words of caution: be careful how you are living your life. This is very simple yet wise advice. Wisdom is a lifestyle; you must live it out on a daily basis, not just some of the time.

There was a time when I wasn't living exactly how God wanted me to. It was at that time I wanted to get married and have children. I didn't know what I was to do: marry the woman I'd been in and out of a relationship with, or pursue Felicity, a woman I was acquainted with as a friend? I knelt down and prayed, "God, I don't know what to do. I'm a coward. Should I continue in this relationship or wait on you for the right one to come? Please, Lord, give me a sign and I will follow through with your will for my life."

Two days later the prayer was answered. I ended up single and open to a new relationship with Felicity. I've now been faithfully married to Felicity for twenty years. At the time I was at a crossroads and I didn't want to live as unwise, so I gave it to God, and he answered my call.

Know Your Limits

The philosopher Aristotle famously said, "Know thyself." I think the principle of taking a step back and gaining perspective is what Aristotle and the apostle Paul are getting at. Be wise. In other words, know your limits.

Understand how you function best and what you need. If you need to take a brief vacation once a quarter, then do so. If you need to rest on the seventh day of the week, do it. Don't be a fool. Be wise and soulish!

New York pastor Dr. Timothy Keller offers some great advice on the importance of taking time off in order to maintain a healthy work-life balance:

> Thus Sabbath is about more than external rest of the body; it is about inner rest of the soul. We need rest from the anxiety and strain of our overwork, which is really an attempt to justify ourselves—to gain the money or the status or the reputation we think we have to have. Avoiding overwork requires deep rest in Christ's finished work for your salvation (Hebrews 4:1–10). Only then will you be able to "walk away" regularly from your vocational work and rest.
>
> Sabbath is the key to getting this balance, and Jesus identifies himself as the Lord of the Sabbath (Mark 2:27–28)—the Lord of Rest! Jesus urges us, "Come to me, all you who are weary and burdened, and I will give you rest. Take my yoke upon you and learn from me, for I am gentle and humble in heart, and you will find rest for your souls" (Matthew 11:28–29). One of

the great blessings of the gospel is that he gives you rest that no one else will.[1]

Dr. Keller touches on a key element in our discussion. He suggests that the only way we can truly find rest is to do so in God. That doesn't mean that we simply mumble a prayer when things get bad. It means recognizing that God created work and he created rest. God wants us, therefore, to balance them both.

What's so great about the verse in the book of Matthew that Keller refers to is that Jesus tells us to get beside him and let him carry the load. When you yoke two animals together they work together under that yoke—their mutual strength is harnessed to do the work. Imagine the implication here. Jesus says that his yoke is easy, his burden light (Matthew 11:30). I wonder why— maybe it's because he's God! In any case, getting rest from God when the entire world is shouting, "Go, go, go!" is a refreshing thought. And that's the point.

The world as we know it must come to a halt as we slide into a re-centering of sorts. This time of rest is what Jesus is referring to. He built a day of rest into creation so that we could find our sanity again. One rabbi wrote this about the Sabbath rest:

Make the Sabbath an eternal monument of the knowledge and sanctification of God, both in the center of your busy public life and in the peaceful retreat of your domestic hearth. For six days cultivate the earth and rule it. . . . But the seventh is the Sabbath of the Lord thy God. . . . Let [a man] therefore realize that the Creator of old is the living God of today, [that He] watches every man and every human effort, to see how man uses or abuses the world loaned to him and the forces bestowed upon him, and that He is the sole architect to Whom every man has to render an account of his week's labors.[2]

Notice how the rabbi balances and recognizes the roles. We have time to do our work and to do it to our utmost. But we must never forget that part of the week should be entirely given to resting in God's peace.

Pastor Gordon MacDonald noted how we all need the Sabbath rest in order to step out of our own ambition and find our center once more. "True rest," wrote MacDonald, "is happening when we pause regularly amidst daily routines to sort out the truths and commitments by which we are living."[3] MacDonald's book *Ordering Your Private World* offers great advice in the area of rest, and I think here he really gets at the meat of what's being achieved when we take time to evaluate, refocus, and go.

In football both the offense and defense huddle up before the offense runs a play. It's a small break in the game. In that time, as the coaches evaluate what's going on from play to play, the quarterback can take a second to refocus the team before they run another play. The huddle gives the team a chance to make sure they're on the right mission, which is to win the game.

What's your mission in life? Are you taking time to huddle up and evaluate, focus, and go?

If we keep going in life, without ever stepping back for rest and perspective, we'll be driven toward ambition and greed. It's in the times of quiet, rest, and reflection that we find our deepest strength—a strength that does not come from us, but from God. Isaiah 30:15 says, "In quietness and trust is your strength." Don't miss out on gaining the strength of God that can only come from rest.

JOY COMES FROM TRIALS

When we go through a trial in life, we tend to search for a way out of it. But we often don't realize that the solution is right in front of us. God promises us that he will never leave us or abandon us. If we can remember this truth when we experience the friction that life brings, then we will not allow anger or bitterness or despair to overtake us.

I love the Bible verse that says we should be "quick to listen, slow to speak and slow to become angry" (James 1:19). This bit of wisdom can protect us during a trial. Instead of reacting to the trial, our first response should be to *wait*. We should first ask God for his strength and wisdom for how to deal with the circumstance at hand.

But this is, typically, not our first response. We are human and we tend to react first and seek wisdom later. What if our first response to the obstacles in our lives was to ask God for *his* perspective, to search for his higher meaning within the trial? If we could respond like this, then perhaps we would understand and adopt this perspective. Maybe we would come through our trials more quickly. Notice how James frames our trials:

> Consider it pure joy, my brothers and sisters, when-
> ever you face trials of many kinds, because you know
> that the testing of your faith produces perseverance.
> Let perseverance finish its work so that you may be
> mature and complete, not lacking anything. . . . Blessed
> is the one who perseveres under trial because, having
> stood the test, that person will receive the crown of
> life that the Lord has promised to those who love
> him. (James 1:2–4, 12)

How can James ask us to consider the tests and challenges of life as "pure joy"? That's what people asked me when Christian passed away. Some people had difficulty understanding our perspective. But the only way for Felicity and me to be able to overcome this great obstacle in life was to take a breath, allow ourselves appropriate time to grieve, and seek God's plan in it all.

Yes, it's much easier said than done. But this is when the discipline of taking regular times of rest (like we just talked about) comes into play. If we are daily taking time to rejuvenate, keeping balance in our work and family lives, then when something really hard comes our way, our first response will be to take time away and find that quiet place where God can speak to us in our time of greatest need.

Parenting, for example, is a tough job. There are times when every parent faces a child (or multiple children) who pushes him or her to the limit. Once past that limit it's very easy to flip out. But sometimes, when we listen rather than react, we find that just because we're the parent doesn't mean we have all the answers. We're not always right.

When we simply calm down and take a breath, we gain perspective. Then we're able to say, "Okay, God, how *should* I react?" Our wrath doesn't erupt, we don't get ourselves into trouble with our spouse, and we don't yell at our children. A benefit, in this scenario, from not reacting in our anger can be the healthy maturing of a child.

Asking God for a good solution can, then, provide us with healthy benefits. We just need to stop, not react, and listen.

Losing Christian was the most difficult trial I've ever faced. My reaction, however, was not an anomaly, as some may think. It stemmed from years of spiritual strength training. I don't say this to puff myself up. Rather, I say it to honor God. It's only through his strength that I was able to face a trial that could have ruined me and our family.

Because I had, up to the day I lost Christian, spent consistent time away from the daily grind of friction and trials, when the greatest trial of all came my way, I sought God *first*.

THE SECRET IS . . . THERE IS NO SECRET

If you choose to persevere, there is always a way. When you think you can't go further in life, God provides an answer. I teach my own children this truth as often as possible.

Randall II, Vashti, and Grace compete in the high jump with our track team. After they jump about seven times they think they have nothing left—maybe one jump, tops. But I coach them up: "You have at least seven more jumps left in you."

The other jumpers hear me coaching my kids and they begin to doubt their own strength because they view my jumpers as having another seven good jumps left. And after my jumpers hear my little speech, they jump and are surprised at how much energy they *do* have left.

I'll give them a lollipop or a power bar or half a bottle of Gatorade almost as a placebo to get their minds believing they can still perform at a high level. But really, it's a mental game! You have to win the mental game to perform at the level you are capable of competing.

The mental game is also coached through our training, which incorporates friction as a huge piece of the puzzle. Prior to high jumping at practice we tire the legs out through running 2 x 500 meters up a hill. Then we run 2 x 400 meters up a hill, and then plyometrics drills that exhaust the legs. After that we perform our high jumping. So in essence my runners are trained to have strength at the end of their jumping.

Our minds affect our bodies in ways we find difficult to understand. But if we can train our minds to believe that when our strength is fading we can pull more from another reservoir, we can be unstoppable not only on the track or on the football field but especially in life.

"Mental toughness is many things," said famous Packers' coach

Vince Lombardi. "It is humility because it behooves all of us to remember that simplicity is the sign of greatness and meekness is the sign of true strength. Mental toughness is spartanism with qualities of sacrifice, self-denial, and dedication. It is fearlessness, and it is love." Lombardi believed that mental toughness was character in action.

That definition connects who we are on the inside to who we are on the outside. It connects our soulish aspect with our physical attributes. Just because you're six foot two and weigh 225 pounds and run a 4.4 forty-yard dash doesn't automatically qualify you as someone who is mentally tough. Sometimes it's the five-foot-four, 160-pound running back who deserves the scholarship to a top Division 1 university. It's often his heart's desire that proves him to be what a coach is looking for out of a player. Big things can come in small packages, right?

If you lack self-discipline or humility or meekness, you will struggle to persevere because you will constantly be worried about yourself and will easily sing the woe-is-me song when given the chance.

What about the trial you're going through today? You're facing bankruptcy or foreclosure; you're staring down divorce or your children are giving you fits. How will your inner strength inform your actions?

Have you taken time to step away from your burdens to recharge yourself, giving yourself time to evaluate and reevaluate before acting?

What are you relying on today to help you through this trial? Do you need someone to come alongside you—someone whose yoke is easy and burden is light?

Perseverance begins with taking that first step. What are you waiting for?

CHAPTER 6
REFLECTION QUESTIONS

What is your own personal definition of perseverance?

———

*In general, are you a persevering kind of person? Or
do you struggle with hanging in there? Explain.*

———

*Do you consistently power down in order to power up? What is your
favorite way of doing so? How do you feel it helps you to persevere?*

———

*What's something you do that you know negatively
affects your ability to persevere? Why do you do it?
How has it affected situations? Be honest!*

———

*Think of an especially difficult time in your life. Did you
persevere, or did you throw in the towel? What was the end
result? Do you wish you had done things differently?*

———

PRINCIPLE 3
WATCHING THE GAME FROM THE TUNNEL

PATIENCE ON AND OFF THE FIELD

The grass that is here today and gone tomorrow does not require much time to mature. A big oak tree that lasts for generations requires much more time to grow and mature.

—HENRY BLACKABY

At the beginning of my football career, I said no to playing quarterback at USC. I had several reasons, though it still seems like an odd decision when I think about it now. But I wanted to play right away and the likelihood of that happening at USC was slim, based on the players who were enrolled on the team. I wanted to show what I could do *now*.

So in 1981 I accepted a scholarship to UNLV to play football. When I arrived at UNLV my brother was there as well. That made it special; we ended up rooming together. That first year I played on the junior varsity squad. Yes, we had one back then—I wasn't ready to play varsity yet. Then in 1982 I heard a rumor that they wanted to redshirt me for my sophomore year. To be redshirted means that you sit out a year—which is supposed to help your development—and you retain that year of eligibility.

I wasn't going for that idea.

I'd signed with UNLV because they had three senior quarterbacks, and I wanted a chance to play as soon as they left. But at the start of my sophomore year, after all the seniors had graduated, I was still listed as the fourth-string quarterback, and I was not happy about it. I had turned down USC to attend UNLV because I knew I could play by my sophomore year.

Sure enough, they had me scheduled to redshirt that year. I insisted I was not going to redshirt and I told my coaches so. They told me that it would be good for me; I could play a fifth year and I'd still make it to the NFL and attain a degree by then.

That simply wasn't in my heart. I had set my goals to become the starter right away. Many didn't know, but after my mother died my freshman year, I had to do it for her. My goals were set, and I wasn't taking no for an answer. I had to be the starting quarterback for Mom . . . and for me.

The first game we played that year was against BYU. Steve Young was their quarterback at the time. They beat us 27–0! During the game, a couple of the coaches and players said, "Hey, let Randall play." After all, we hadn't scored any points. It couldn't hurt.

I'd watched the scoreboard: BYU 7, UNLV 0. Then BYU 14, UNLV 0. Then BYU 21, UNLV 0. I just knew I was going to get an opportunity to play.

Finally, BYU 27, UNLV 0. Game over.

The frustration began to settle in as players asked me, "Why couldn't they give you a few minutes to prove yourself?" I had to keep the tears from coming down my face in their presence. It was an awful time. I wanted to prove to Mom I could do it.

But the door didn't open that game.

I was upset, and in my arrogance, I thought that I would just walk off the field right then and there and transfer to USC.

But after the BYU shellacking we had a bye week (a week off). The coaches let it be known to the team and around the school that they were going to reevaluate the quarterback position and that even fourth-string Randall Cunningham was going to have a chance to play.

I had to consider this new opportunity. In my pride and anger I wanted to leave and play for USC. But I needed to calm down. I needed to be patient, stick it out, and see what might come from the evaluation period.

The coaches told all four of us that they were evaluating the position and that we'd better work hard during the week of practice. So I committed myself to performing to the best of my ability, no matter the odds. I worked even harder to eliminate my mental and physical mistakes. I went deeper into the playbook. I wanted to know more than the coaching staff.

I gave it my best shot so I wouldn't be tempted to transfer somewhere else. I felt confident that if I could just focus and perform, then the coaches would see my potential and perhaps I'd become the starter.

All four quarterbacks practiced hard the following week. The coaches called us into their offices on Saturday to inform us of their decision.

"Guys, we've thought long and hard about this. We have

watched each of you closely this week. We've documented your statistics and—"

"Coach, just tell us who it is," one of the senior quarterbacks interrupted.

He was right; we just wanted to know. At that point we were *all* ready to walk out of the room and transfer to other schools.

The coaches kept saying, "Well, we've given everyone a chance."

It was driving me nuts!

Finally, the head coach said matter-of-factly, "Randall Cunningham is the starting quarterback."

If I remember correctly, one of the players slid down in his seat in agitation, another one congratulated me, and another walked out of the room, upset and hurt. I'm sure that was a hard pill to swallow—the disappointment of no longer having control over their future football career. That's difficult to stomach.

Coach made it clear that whoever they picked was going to be the quarterback for the remainder of the season. When he said that, peace came over me like never before: the hard work, the dedication, the *patience* had paid off. I would now be able to bless Mom.

I was now the starting quarterback at UNLV—as a sophomore. This is what I'd envisioned for myself.

My first game was against New Mexico and all they did was

blitz the whole game. I was baptized by fire in Lobo stadium that week as a college starting quarterback. It was on. I went 3-7 that year, but I never looked back.

PATIENCE—THE VIRTUE I LEARNED THE HARD WAY

There was a time in my NFL career when I prayed for patience. I wasn't a patient man. Sure, there were flashes of patience, but overall I struggled with this virtue. So I asked God for it.

"Oh, God," I prayed, "give me patience!"

Be careful what you pray for.

Shortly after I made that prayer we opened our season with a one o'clock game in Green Bay, Wisconsin. The Philadelphia Eagles against the Packers. There were high expectations for us that year. We were expected to win the conference. It was the post–Buddy Ryan era, and Rich Kotite was our coach.

In the first quarter of that game we struggled on offense. I approached the coach. "Coach, let's throw a couple of deep balls to Barnett and Williams. Maybe we can get something going or at least a pass interference call." I was trying to think of a way to jolt the offense into a rhythm—to gain some kind of momentum. After all, Lambeau Field, the home of the Packers, isn't the easiest venue to get things going. If we didn't rattle ourselves out of the funk, we'd lose for sure.

So on the next series Coach acquiesced and called the play I wanted. But Lambeau was rocking. It was insanely loud—like we were playing next to an airfield full of fighter jets about to take off. The Packers fans were whipped into a frenzy. It's hard to explain that kind of atmosphere unless you've been to a game there. Even more so, it's a whole different experience when you're the opposing quarterback under center on the field.

Despite the deafening crowd noise, we were still able to get the ball hiked on time. As I surveyed the developing play from my position in the pocket, eyes downfield locking in a target, a defensive lineman named Bryce Paup—he was six foot five and 247 pounds—broke through and hit me square in my knee. I bent forward, then I bent backward . . . while my knee stayed locked.

Bam! I was on the turf thrashing around in pain. The hit blew my medial collateral ligament off the bone and tore off my posterior cruciate ligament as well.

At first the crowd cheered because it was an incomplete pass. But then there was a collective gasp in the stadium when everyone realized I had suffered what appeared to be a major injury. I lay there squirming while the stadium quieted. To this day I remember that pain. I remember that hit. But I also remember who called that play: me. I had begged Coach to call that play and he allowed me to call it.

When you suffer a major injury like that, your mind races from the pain to thoughts like, *Oh, man, it's over . . . I'm done for the season . . . Could this end my career?* As I lay there in pain, thinking awful thoughts, the trainers came out and tested my knee. It was in bad shape, just kind of flopping over to the left.

They strapped me so nothing could move and placed me on the cart. The fans applauded that I was apparently okay and able to get off the field. But as the cart went into the tunnel the thought that kept playing over and over in my mind was, *Well, I'm the one who kept praying for patience.* I wonder if those were my thoughts or if that was God's voice in my head saying, *Randall, remember, you asked me for patience. I've allowed this to happen to you so you can learn patience in the most real and meaningful way possible.*

All I could say was, "Well, thank you, God. Thank you."

After an MRI and more testing, the doctors determined that I had to have surgery. They did a complete reconstruction, using cadaver ligaments to repair the damage. When I spoke to my orthopedic surgeon, Dr. Clarence Shields, I asked him if it was possible to replace my medial collateral and posterior ligaments with ligaments from the late Olympic track star Jesse Owens. I wanted to return to the NFL faster and stronger than ever. We laughed, but he didn't realize it was a very serious question. I was on my road to recovery.

Since I hadn't yet married and started a family, following the surgery I stayed in Marina Del Rey at the Ritz–Carlton all by myself. Former Super Bowl great Ronnie Lott stopped by and spent a moment with me. "Hey, man, it's going to be all right. Just wanted you to know we're thinking about you." Ronnie was an angel that day and didn't even realize it. I had been in the tank mentally.

I was doing okay, but it's a humbling experience when you're a professional athlete and you're reduced to hobbling around on crutches. I had to take baths with my leg sticking straight out at a ninety-degree angle in the air to keep it from getting wet. Whenever I'd let my leg down, I felt an incredible pain throbbing in the reconstructed part. I refused to take pain medication at that point because I wanted to work through the pain. And as I struggled through the pain and the humiliation I remember praying over and over for *patience*.

But weaning yourself off morphine is no joke. Every night in the hotel I'd wake up two or three times in a cold sweat. I would perspire so badly I'd have to use towels to dry myself off. I'd lie there wrapped in towels just trying to sleep.

During the days I'd go to the mall and walk around on my crutches just to keep my strength up. The doctors told me it would take about nine months to fully recuperate. I stayed away from the Eagles organization for one of those months, rehabilitating on my own.

Finally, I returned to the team for the remainder of my rehab—the team was now already into the meat of the season. I don't remember my first game back on the sidelines, but I do remember Coach Kotite insisting that I leave the sidelines and go into another area to watch the game, since I wasn't an active-roster player. I had a deep desire to be part of the team and root for my teammates. After all, I was one of the team leaders and I wanted to continue serving and leading in any way I could.

Coach said I could stand in the tunnel.

The tunnel?

That was hard.

Imagine that you're the starting quarterback for a premier NFL franchise and then you endure a season-ending injury. Immediately you're cut off from everything because you're in surgery. Then comes rehab, where you're trying your best to do everything you can to get back to being a contributor. It wasn't your fault—the injury was out of your hands. But your position must be filled and suddenly you're relegated to standing off at a distance—not allowed to stand on the sidelines with your teammates.

If ever I felt like I was on the outside looking in, it was during that time of my life. They were all on the sidelines and I was watching the game from the tunnel.

That was a hard pill to swallow. But God was true to his word in teaching me patience. I missed the entire season, and during that time God let me know that I had no control over anything but my rehabilitation.

By the beginning of the next season I was wearing a knee brace and playing again. I played with the knee brace on for half the season. It truly gave me confidence to do what I had to without worrying about being injured again. The mental component of rehabilitating a knee injury is just as important as the physical, in my opinion.

Last year I heard several sports commentators discussing Adrian "AP" Peterson's knee surgery and rehab. One of the commentators was former NFL All-Pro running back Eddie George. Eddie commented on how surprised he was at AP's mental recovery, citing that the mental aspect was taking much longer to overcome than the physical aspect. He talked about how many running backs tend to favor their knee and even protect it as they cut through holes at the line of scrimmage.

I knew what he meant. The mental aspect for me was wrapped up in my time away from the game and the process of getting healthy. I simply felt I didn't need my brace anymore. I ended up rushing for over five hundred yards that season. People were amazed at how well I played after what seemed like a career-ending injury. I believe I played so well and had no problems with my knee because God blessed my patience and the hard work it took to overcome the injury. To this day I have no problem at all with that knee, and I'm about fifty years young.

I really believe that if we learn to be patient and take the time to overcome the obstacles that come our way in life, then we'll find that there's blessing on the other side.

WHY WILDERNESS TIMES ARE GOOD

I've read accounts of people from the first-century church who would spend months, even years, in the desert to get closer to God. In the desert the typical cultural distractions are gone; it's just you and the elements and God.

My wilderness time was my season watching my teammates from the tunnel. During those days it felt as though no one cared about Randall Cunningham. I was just another fan who cheered on the Eagles. I felt as though there was no longer a need for me to be on the team and that they could move on without me. *Who is Randall Cunningham but a washed-up nothing?* That was the kind of thinking that ran through my mind.

But it was all good, because it caused me to become a better person and teammate. I realized that it wasn't all about me, or what I thought or wanted—a humbling experience for anyone to learn. When all you can do is hobble around on crutches, you're forced to rely on God. I guess this is how God thought it best to teach me patience, to teach me to rely on him and not on my own ability.

Sometimes in life, we find ourselves in a barren place. For you it might be a mental or spiritual wilderness where you feel like you're working through something all alone, like the pain of losing a loved one or the betrayal of a friend. You can't talk to anyone about it—it's just you and your thoughts. Whatever your wilderness time may be now or whatever it has been, I believe those times can bring great moments of personal epiphany and healing and can also cause you to seek God like you've never done before.

In the Bible the apostle Paul experienced a wilderness time. Prior to finding God he was a Jewish teacher of the law. Called Saul, he was smart and was working his way into becoming a great and well-known teacher. During the early stages of the Christian church, he actually persecuted those who followed and believed in Christ.

Then he ran into God.

The famous story of Saul on the Damascus Road is a favorite of mine. God reveals himself to Saul, tells him that Jesus really was his Son, and instructs Saul to go and tell the world about it. That was a turning point for Saul, when God set him off in a new life direction.

What did Paul do after this supernatural encounter with God? Did he go tell all of Damascus? Did he tweet about it? Did he even seek counsel from his superiors? No. After a couple of weeks recuperating from his encounter with God, Paul spent three years in the Arabian wilderness. We really don't know what he did during this time. I like to believe that he spent time with God, preparing his mind and body for the task ahead. Later in Paul's ministry he endured beatings and shipwrecks and all kinds of intense treatment from people. And his time spent alone with God in the desert would definitely have helped prepare him for those times.

My wilderness time was that year of rehab. Once I detached from my normal routine of life and football, I was able to see things more clearly. It was during that time that God actually showed me, through my physical injury, that patience requires trust—and one way to trust is to endure something difficult and find yourself still intact on the other side of it.

VIRTUES FOUND IN PATIENCE

There's a scene in the Bible where parents brought their children to Jesus so that he would bless them. But Jesus' disciples got annoyed and tried to keep the children from him.

People were bringing little children to Jesus for him to place his hands on them, but the disciples rebuked them. When Jesus saw this, he was indignant. He said to them, "Let the little children come to me, and do not hinder them, for the kingdom of God belongs to such as these. Truly I tell you, anyone who will not receive the kingdom of God like a little child will never enter it." And he took the children in his arms, placed his hands on them and blessed them. (Mark 10:13–16)

Jesus used the situation to teach his disciples. Notice he said that unless we come to him like a child, we cannot enter the kingdom of God. Some pastors and teachers use this passage to talk about how important it is to possess childlike faith. But Jesus is not talking about a childlike innocence with regard to faith in God. Rather, he's talking about a trust and dependency that mirrors that of a child.

Think about how children depend on their parents for *everything*. They rely on their father and mother for shelter, for food, for safety. They rely on their parents for love and for general care. Toddlers will walk off a table if their parents tell them to; they intrinsically trust their parents. They can't help but trust.

In other words, children have an unwavering trust.

When we talk about learning patience we are not just talking about playing the waiting game. Patience is like an umbrella.
Beneath that umbrella two characteristics stand ready to invite
you in from the rain.

Dependency

When I watched from the tunnel as my team played on the field,
I had to ask myself a tough question: was I more dependent upon
my athletic ability and status as an NFL quarterback than I was
on God?

Too many times in our culture we relegate faith to the
margin. We mention God when things go great and we pray
before meals, and we may even attend a Sunday church service
because it's the right thing to do. But faith isn't something we
do; it's a relationship cultivated over time with God.

The New Testament writer John the Beloved referred to this
kind of life as an *abiding life*. He calls Jesus the vine and us the
branches. If we abide in Jesus, he will abide in us. A branch is
utterly dependent upon the sustenance of the vine. Without it,
the branch will wither and die (John 15).

Sitting alone in the Ritz-Carlton bathtub, standing alone in
the tunnel of a football stadium, and spending hours in the gym
and on the practice field rehabbing my knee taught me that
patience is built by having a dependency on God and abiding in

him. The less I tried to rely upon my own strength and instead leaned on God, the calmer I became.

In the wilderness times of life it's easy to fall into despair. We tend to fall apart when we find ourselves in a place away from the masses, alone with our thoughts. Who are we in those times? It's in those moments where we, again, come up against the "What if . . . ?" thoughts. *What if I quit my job? What if I drop out of school? What if I never get married? What if I never see my kids again after the divorce?* We're each faced with the temptation to turn inward and fall into the pit of despair.

Or we can choose to stand and continue relying on God and not our own strength.

Remember how I mentioned that when I arrived home and found out what had happened to my son, I didn't (and still don't) really know how I was able to power through my own feelings and even think of my family? God was carrying me at that point. I was utterly dependent upon him. And when I needed him most, he not only answered my prayers, but he reached down and carried me when I couldn't stand.

Humility

The second characteristic, humility, also stands beneath the umbrella of patience, waiting to show us a better way to think and act toward others. The famous South African missionary and pastor Andrew Murray wrote, "Humility is simply the disposition which prepares the soul for living on trust." Humility and dependency (trust) are linked arm in arm under the umbrella of patience.

In our culture, people do not prize humility as much as they value self-glorification. Reggie White was a humble man, yet he was also confident. Can you be both? Yes, I believe that true humility shows itself to be a disposition that clings to truth. When we understand our current circumstance and the people involved in that circumstance, as well as how we can contribute to that circumstance, I think we finally understand humility.

It would be false humility for me to act like my performance on the football field surprised me. On the other hand, it would be pompous to boast about myself in a "Look what I can do!" kind of way. I find and show true humility when I embrace my ability in light of the circumstance: I'm a professional football player and can do certain things with a football because that is what I've been trained to do. What I do and how I *present* that ability is where either humility comes forward or arrogance speaks out. If I use my ability to serve my teammates, if I discuss the games afterward with the press in a way that shows thoughtful insight and joy—rather than praising myself—then my disposition reflects humility.

If I seize the truth of my ability and showcase it, if I boast about it in a haughty manner, then I've crossed the line of humility, past self-confidence and into arrogance. Reggie White knew what he could do on a football field, but he didn't let that truth inflate his head. He had fun with it and used his ability and influence to serve others.

When I was sidelined for that year I was knocked down a peg. In the span of a play I was reduced from starting quarterback to injured reserve. I learned humility during that waiting period. I learned how to wait on God and his timing. I learned that humble people are patient—they do not let outside circumstances affect the steady nature of their journey. They take adversity in stride, realize their place within that adversity (humility), and continue to do the same things they always did, working toward their goal with renewed resolve.

PATIENT AS GOD SHAPES ME

The other day I walked into my closet and picked up one of Christian's shirts. (I keep many of his clothes hanging in my closet.) I smelled it just to see if his scent was still on the clothes. Then I started to cry and in my spirit I let God know that I miss my son's presence in my life. I miss his smile. I miss him doing his little push-ups and sit-ups in the house. I miss everything about him. My family and I are still in a season where we're trying to get through the reality of life without him.

But Christian is gone now, and no amount of grieving can bring him back. We are utterly helpless in this process; we have no control over it. Continue living—that is all we can do.

Still, it's hard sometimes not to think about the "what would have been." When we have children, the older they grow, the more we see qualities of ourselves in them. That excites us as parents in a way that is hard to explain but that any parent can understand. Not a pride-of-life sort of way, but more of a "What, O Lord, will this child accomplish?" way.

We were beginning to see glimpses of ourselves in Christian and were excited to see what he would achieve, and our minds would fast-forward daily on thoughts in that regard. An immense amount of joy and pride would well up in me when I would think of the potential accolades bestowed upon Christian. I so desired for him—as I do with all my children—to surpass any-thing that I had done in life or in sports.

That feeling is all part of the oneness you experience with your children. You want the best for them; you want them to go beyond what you've accomplished. You want them to use the paths you've blazed in order to go deeper into the beauty and wonder of life. You want them to have more than you had.

Then . . . take all that and delete it in an instant. And what are you left with?

You're left with an ongoing pain that ebbs and flows in seasons. At first we grieved the initial loss of our boy. We dealt with shame and guilt and the sheer gut-wrenchingness of the whole situation. Then we celebrated his homegoing, tears mingling with laughter—that same sense as when I lifted his clothes to my face and inhaled.

We passed from that season into a season of waiting. Now we are waiting on God for our sustenance and strength to continue on day to day. Enduring and waiting and persevering are inextricably linked and are all necessary to come out on the other side of pain.

Yet life doesn't just stop and wait for you to regain your footing after something tragic happens. Felicity and I are now a few years out from the tragedy and we have responsibilities we must continue to fulfill. We must continue to lead our family. We must continue to remain effective in our community, leading in any way we can. I lead a church congregation. I have a voice of leadership in the Las Vegas and the greater Nevada region. All this must continue.

Yet Christian is with me and my wife and children daily. His picture is on my phone, on my laptop computer, and on my desk. Daily his legacy lives within us—his life, now in a way only God could formulate, molds us into the people and leaders and family members and friends God wants us to be.

The Bible says God's ways are not our ways (Isaiah 55:8–9). Certainly, it may seem odd for God to use the death of my son to help form others' lives, but to me that speaks to the type of person Christian was. What a special boy. And every life that crossed into Christian's is touched deeply in some special way—most of all the lives of my family.

I believe one day we will see Christian again in heaven. God is a good God, and he will reunite us in the most perfect of places. How fitting. It is that hope—the hope of "someday"—that propels us into the next day, week, and year. It is the ultimate lesson on patience, you see. But as with the smaller things, this refines us more each day into the sons and daughters God wants us to be, dependent on him. And we are grateful not only for his strength but for the lesson. God continues to shape me, a forty-nine-year-old dad and coach and husband, into a better, more patient man through the legacy of my son.

He can absolutely do the same for you.

CHAPTER 7
REFLECTION QUESTIONS

*Detail a time in your life when you willingly
practiced patience to achieve a goal—spiritual, mental,
physical, or other. What were the results?*

━━━

*Now detail a time in your life when God unexpectedly "forced"
you to practice patience. How were you brought to that place?
Were you successful or unsuccessful in practicing patience?*

━━━

*How much harder is it to be patient when the situation
is not to your liking? Do you feel closer to and more
dependent on God in those times? Or do you struggle
with anger or disappointment? Explain.*

━━━

*Think of a time in your life when you practiced patience. Has
it had a lasting impression on what kind of person you are?
If so, how? Are you glad you went through the experience?*

━━━

*If there was a lesson in patience you'd want to
teach your loved ones, what would it be?*

━━━

8

PRINCIPLE 4
LIMPING BACK TO THE HUDDLE

GRIEVE, GET MAD, MOVE ON

When the door of happiness closes, another opens. But often times we look so long at the closed door that we don't see the one which has been opened for us.

—ALEXANDER GRAHAM BELL

If you get hurt, then deal with it. And I don't say that with grit in my teeth or a harsh tone. I mean, seriously, deal with it or it will linger forever.

I remember when I began to work as an evangelist years ago, I would go out to share my testimony. It was my first time really ministering with a group of people. We'd go into a church and lead worship, and then I'd share my testimony.

Well, I didn't know what ministry was like on the road, but I began to deal with different personalities. I remember it had been tough on me that season of evangelism. A few people were not getting along, and I tried to minister to fix the problem, only to be caught off guard by their resistance.

I actually ended up offended and hurt in my spirit. I decided to call my pastor for a little counseling. "Pastor John," I said, "people are talking behind my back and rebelling against me. I just needed a little encouragement."

"Randall, it's going to be okay. Just keep your head up," he said. "It's not your fault." I really was looking for him to baby me.

"Pastor," I said, "why is this happening? I thought everyone in church was supposed to be perfect."

"We're all growing," he replied. "Randall, welcome to ministry. Get over it."

I was shocked, but later I understood what he meant. I needed to have tough skin in ministry. Not only are we up against issues needing solutions, but the enemy is against *us* as well. I didn't get the hug I needed that day, but I did get what God wanted me to have: a taste of reality. Ministry is not for the faint of heart.

Life is going to hurt us; it's inevitable. But how will we respond? How will you? How will I?

YOU WILL HURT

When I injured my knee playing the Green Bay Packers, I could not ignore the pain. The injury hobbled me. And if I hadn't seen the appropriate doctors and specialists, I would not have healed or rehabilitated correctly.

I took the time I needed—that my body demanded—in order to heal so that I could return to the field and be the same pre-injury Randall *physically*, but a stronger Randall *spiritually*.

Just like a football player has to leave the game when he's injured, sometimes we need to leave the field of life for a few plays before we hop back into the action. But during our time away, we need to deal with the pain appropriately so that we can return stronger spiritually.

I've talked to some people about my son's passing and they sit stunned at how I was able to overcome the pain of the situation and talk about it with such a calm demeanor. They marvel at my resiliency. As a pastor and a person who does his utmost to follow God, I tell people that it was and still is God's strength that brought me through such a hard time and continues to sustain me. I'm only able to talk about my son going home because of the strength that God provides.

But just because I can talk about the tragedy now doesn't mean I was able to do that right away. I took the time I needed to grieve, and my wife and children took the time they needed. If we hadn't given ourselves permission to grieve, we couldn't have moved on.

IT'S OKAY TO GRIEVE

During my first year of college, my brother and I received news that our mother wasn't doing well and we needed to visit her. I loved my mother, Mable Cunningham, very much.

I had left college just for a weekend to go see how she was doing—my brother, Bruce, and I just wanted to be near her as she suffered through cancer. When we arrived at the hospital not only was she unresponsive but she also had tubes coming out of her every whichway.

I remember I walked out of her room to help take care of one of the nephews, and it was then she passed away. When I returned to her room they told me what had happened. Bruce ran out of the hospital and into the parking lot screaming and crying. And I ran with him, as younger brothers do. Bruce was my example and I looked to him to see how he was going to respond. Bruce let it out.

And there, in the hospital parking lot in Goleta, California, we mourned in the open air. We were hurting out loud, as it were. We really didn't know what to do or how to respond. Is there even a response for something as grievous as losing your mother?

That vision of Bruce running into the parking lot has stuck with me all these years and reminds me that there's a time to grieve. We're not supposed to deny pain. The appropriate response to losing a loved one is grief—open grief. And there is no right or wrong way to do it. As we all discover when death comes to our loved ones, in that moment we really don't know what to do or how to respond. The only language we understand at that moment is the language of weeping. The only thing that feels right is sobbing.

I understand that people are wired differently. Some people automatically turn inward when tragedy or hard times come. Some people lash out. Neither extreme is good. What we should seek, however, is clear and open recognition of our feelings. Then we should give ourselves permission to feel, and feel deeply. It's okay to cry about a loss or a betrayal. It's okay to get mad; feelings of abandonment and bitterness well up in us when we experience these different kinds of deep hurt. It's how God made us.

A comforting thought for me to reflect on in times of heavy grief is the scene from the Bible when Jesus finally arrived at Bethany to visit the grave of one of his closest friends, Lazarus. This scene is thick with meaning that I won't go into right now, but when Jesus first arrived and saw the pain and loss in Lazarus's sisters, Mary and Martha, he was cut to the core. Here we find the shortest verse in all of Scripture: "Jesus wept" (John 11:35).

How comforting to read about how the Son of God reacted to the loss of a friend! It's okay to cry. It's okay for doubt to swirl in your mind.

It's okay . . . it's okay.

The danger lies not in those feelings but in the fact that if those feelings remain—if they linger on and on and take root in your heart—then negativity can set in and your behavior will shift from grief to despair. And when you give in to despair, you live void of all hope.

That's a dark place to be, but you can do something about it. You can grieve, get mad, and move on. If you have to tell yourself that that's your progression, then do so. If you have to find someone to watch your behavior and keep you accountable to a proper response to grief and pain, then do so. Do whatever you can to eliminate the possibility of anger or bitterness taking root.

Once we're honest with our feelings and have given our-selves permission to trudge through them for a time, we must then release those feelings. Easier said than done, I know. But here's how we release those feelings. We release them to God and his goodness. What does that mean? How can we release our pain to the goodness of God?

One of God's attributes is goodness. He alone is good. He is the originator of all that is good.

You may be saying, "But Randall, if God is so good, why do bad things still happen?" It's an interesting question, but I think that question comes from a skewed perspective. It's not that bad things happen in the face of a good God and he does nothing. It's that even through the worst of calamities, God can bring about beauty *because* he is so good.

You've heard the saying that God can bring beauty from ashes? It's the same idea behind the phoenix rising from the ashes—new life springs from something that was dead. That is exactly what God does for us. He can bring about complete goodness through the most horrific things. This can be hard to wrap our minds around, but it's the truth. When we give our grief to God's goodness and trust that he is making all things new, we will see something beautiful spring from the hardest obstacles to overcome in this life.

I remember being graveside at Mom's funeral, listening to

the service unfold. As I stood there, a hard lump lodged itself in my throat. It was a lump of pain. I tried choking it down even as I began to cry. I realized my mother wasn't coming back. And while I stood there dealing with the death of my mom, God placed people at my side to comfort me. What a godsend! Those folks were there for this college boy as he wrestled with all the thoughts that come along with losing someone you love so dearly.

When I returned to UNLV after the funeral, one of my coaches, Coach Mims, approached me.

"Randall," he said, "we know you're going through a difficult time right now. If there's anything any one of us can do on the coaching staff or team, let us know. We'll be here for you. We'll help you get through this."

Those words, which can seem insignificant to the person saying them, meant the world to me. Just like there is a time to grieve, there is also a time to be comforted, and you have to *allow* yourself to be comforted. It's true that when you lose someone that close you don't really want to talk about it. You don't like to hear it verbalized. It's too hard to hear. But even though I didn't want to hear about my mom's passing I still needed to hear friends, and in this case my coaches, verbalizing their support for me.

Things didn't get any easier for me that year. Later on I lost my father. You can understand the depth to which I sank in terms of the loss I experienced that year. That year hurt. But when we lost our mother, my brother, Bruce, taught me that it was okay to cry. It was okay to run into a parking lot screaming. I had been given permission to grieve. Grieving doesn't necessarily make the pain more bearable, but it serves as an outlet for the emotion.

In between our mother's and father's passings, Bruce and I lost a good friend to death as well: Tony Gilbert. Tony was a longtime friend of the family who was attending Michigan State on a scholarship. He was a great triple jumper and a fantastic football player; he was destined for the NFL and the Olympics. But we lost him.

Losing Tony was a hard experience. It was bad enough that he was a close friend of our family, but it made it even more difficult knowing that he was so young and had such a promising career in athletics. I could have allowed myself to linger on the tough questions, like *why would God allow such a promising athlete to die?* But that only would have propelled me into thoughts of doubt and confusion.

When loss piles up in your life, like it did in mine that year, how will you respond? Will you suppress the pain, locking it up inside? Or will you give yourself permission to grieve yet still remain grounded in what you know to be true?

GET TO KNOW GOD

The year I lost Mom and Pop and Tony was a tough year. Looking back, I'm thankful for my brother's example of how to deal with pain. I was obviously not as mature as I am now, but what I *know* helped me during that time was taking the opportunity to grieve and being okay with it. My faith then was not what it is now, but that's okay. Life is a process, just like being a leader is a process—there are events and circumstances that shape our entire lives, readying us for the moment where we will need uncommon strength.

For me that moment was the passing of Christian. Although you can never be ready to lose a child, I was prepared, to some extent, for the process of pain, for dealing with it and allowing myself to do that.

We can know how to deal with the process of pain because of past experience, but only our *faith* will be able to sustain us through true tragedy. It's easy when life is going well to underestimate the role faith plays in our daily lives. As a Christian, I believe that we have the opportunity every day to cultivate a relationship with God. But if that relationship goes stale and we go it alone, when tragedy strikes, our heads will spin and doubt will crowd our hearts.

I wear my faith on my sleeve. I don't apologize for it and I don't make excuses for it. It's woven into my fabric as a person—it's in my DNA. So when something bad happens in my life, I give myself permission to hurt and to deal with the pain, but then I look to my faith in God. The peace that passes understanding cannot come from a human being. It comes from the God of peace. It comes from a God who is sovereign—who knows all things and is all-powerful and who understands the pain we feel.

If God created us, doesn't he have all the permission in the world to call us back home to be with him whenever he wants? Does that make him a malevolent God? Does it make him a selfish God? No, it makes him a loving God that he would care so much about us that he wants us with him. When God makes a decision like that, we must realize that it's out of our hands. It's in *his* hands. Where is there a safer place to be?

When death touches our lives, whether it is a friend or our children, we must learn to view it as a growing time. And the only way to do that is to cultivate a relationship with the God of all life.

In a greenhouse, young plants grow in a controlled environment. Over time, however, the grower rolls the ceiling back and allows the cool fall air to drift in over the plants. But each plant sits on a heated floor. Its roots are warm, its soil nourished with water. The cool air from the outside world causes the plant's roots to grow stronger so that the plant can become hardier—

able to withstand colder temperatures. Finally, the plant matures and is able to be planted in the earth where the soil temperature is controlled only by the weather, which is random and sometimes harsh.

Yet through it all, the plant grows because it has weathered the cold before. A loving grower, who knew what was best for the young plant, cultivated it and allowed the harsh cold in at just the right time so that the plant's roots would grow. Because one day the plant would have to be hardy enough to survive the winter cold and the summer drought.

Our relationship with God is not unlike the one between the plant and the grower. He allows things to come into our lives to make our roots hardy, so to speak. Our challenge is in shifting our perspective so that we view prosperity and tragedy through the same lens.

LEARN AN ANCIENT LESSON

The biblical story of Job comes to mind here. It is said that the story of Job is the oldest recorded story in the Bible. The story is full of intense and nearly fantastical scenes. But it is more than a story; it is God's message to us through Job's life.

Job was a prominent businessman who was very successful. He possessed great wealth and influence and was blessed with a large and thriving family. In a blink God allowed all Job had to be taken away—his children tragically lost; his business upended and wealth stolen; his body wracked by sores, ultimately leading him to the brink of despair.

Yet through it all Job did not curse God. He *did* use pretty harsh language and demand vindication. He *did* cry desperately for God to hear him, like you and I do at times in life when things spin out of control. How often have you found yourself praying to God when things go really bad, even though you hadn't prayed in a while? Sooner or later everyone is driven to prayer. That's what life does; it moves us toward God.

But despite Job's methods, God listened to Job's plea and then responded to him. And in the end God helped Job gain perspective by stating his grandeur and omnipotence and ultimate power and control over every created thing. He basically told Job that there's much in this world that we can never understand and we need to be okay with that. Though he despaired, Job recognized God as the giver and the taker in this life. He responded first with the realization that now that he had God's attention he really had nothing to say. His next response was worship.

What I love about God's response to Job is what we don't hear God say. We don't hear, "Now hold it, little man. You're just a human and I'm God. You can't talk to me that way." God is big enough for our cries, for our pleas, and for our outright screaming to be heard and comforted. We are never so far gone in this life to be outside of God's control. We must fight to remember this and to run to God when things happen. We must also remember that when tragedy or extreme times fall upon us or our family members, God can handle our grief and confusion; he can handle our demands on him. He is God.

It's okay to cry. It's okay to grieve. Do you think that God's heart doesn't break because of all the brokenness in our world? He knows that the world pushes in on us, but he will not allow us to be crushed.

Picture Job. There he sat on an ash heap. His clothes were torn because he'd been mourning, and his skin was cut and infected because of the sickness that befell him. And yet, at the end of it all, it was enough just to see God answer him. He was still mourning. His life was still in shambles. But he was comforted.

Comfort is what we strive for when things get tough. But nothing this world offers can give us the comfort we truly need. Only God can do that. We need only cry out for him to comfort us and not let go until we see his face.

This doesn't mean we won't struggle. When I played in the NFL I struggled with losing friends as personnel shifts sent my friends to other teams and new towns. That might sound trivial to some, but it really hurt me deeply. When you're an NFL player, it can be a lonely existence if not for your brothers on the team and their families. The league is certainly a brotherhood, and because football is the ultimate team sport, you bond with the guys you suit up with every week. I remember feeling wounded when a coach wouldn't fight to keep a certain player on the team—especially if it was one of the better players.

You can imagine my frustration when Keith Jackson went to the Packers along with Reggie White. Those were my brothers and they were incredible players, Hall of Fame–caliber players. Reggie was the first big free agent of the modern era, and it hurt to see him go. Keith Byars ended up going to the Patriots. And there I was wondering why we couldn't all just stay on the same team and do something special.

When Buddy Ryan was fired, that cut me. We *played* for Buddy; we loved Buddy. Picture yourself working for an organization for a number of years. You work really hard to be the best, and as you grow into your role you become close to those around you who are working as your team members toward a common goal. You spend so much time with them that you feel they are part of your family. Then they get fired and move to new cities. That was my reality.

My point is that you and I face the reality of the daily grind in our particular work environments. We will face circumstances in our vocations that will hurt us. We may also face situations more personal, within our immediate families, that will cut us deeply as well. We will experience pain and emotional hurt throughout it all, and that's okay.

But what isn't okay is to view those times as the end of the world. It's okay to feel and to work through the hard things, but holding on to those experiences and allowing yourselves to become embittered because of them will eat at us like a cancer. We are most healthy emotionally, I have found, when we identify the things that hurt us, grieve over them, and then bury them in the past.

Yes, the emotional hurt can linger. That's why it's important not to move on simply for the sake of moving on, but to make sure that we have fully dealt with whatever or whoever hurt us.

The lingering effect of my son's passing lives with me daily. But I have dealt with the emotional side of things to where my lingering pain is more like nostalgia—I really miss my son but know he is with God in a much better place. It would be a different ball game if I remained bitter toward God or a family member because of what happened. But I don't, and that's the power of forgiveness and thankfulness and contentment.

IT'S NOT YOUR FAULT

Christian was actually our fifth child. Shortly before he came into our lives, we had discovered we were pregnant for the fourth time. It was a beautiful time in life. Felicity and I were both excited to be having our fourth. We told our other children the news and there was a special buzz in the air.

But later in the pregnancy, at a routine checkup, the doctor discovered that the child's heart wasn't beating. My wife miscarried.

It was a difficult time for both of us. Felicity didn't know how to get through that experience. I remember one day I walked into our room. I didn't know what to say to her; I had never experienced anything in my life similar to this. So I asked her, "Do you want to talk about it?"

"Yes," she said.

I don't think I was supposed to say anything at that point, only listen.

So that's what I did. She began talking about the miscarriage and asked me if there was something she had done wrong. She had been carrying the weight of guilt around with her and it was becoming too heavy to bear. "Of course this isn't your fault," I told her. "This is God's decision."

The reminder that God was in this event in our lives encouraged my wife.

I don't think knowing that God is in something makes the pain any less real. But it does provide perspective. I'm sure there are some reading this who can relate to experiencing a miscarriage, or maybe something similar. I want to encourage you to release that to God. I'm not promising that your pain will subside right away, but I can promise his peace, which passes all understanding. And that kind of peace is more valuable than gold when a circumstance as painful as this arises.

But I want to take it one step further. Yes, I want you to understand and see that God is in control, but I also want you to ask God for forgiveness for blaming yourself. You are not to blame. I think this is one of the main reasons we struggle to move on from pain in our lives: we blame ourselves and are crushed by the weight of guilt. Why do we enjoy blaming ourselves when tragedy strikes? Why do we always look for someone to blame instead of looking for and obtaining the healing that we need to continue on in life?

I think sometimes, in our anger, we can almost curse those we love by yelling at them and saying, "You did this! You're to blame!" Saying something like that can wound people in their spirit and cause them to hold on to the pain for years and years, all the while breaking under the strain of guilt. They hear those words and begin to contemplate, "Well, maybe it was my fault. Maybe I did do it."

I know some people endure tough childhoods and struggle with the guilt of their parents' divorcing or, perhaps, the constant reinforcement of guilt from a parent who did not love them and heaped abuse into their lives. Or perhaps a spouse or boss showered constant blame on them. They spent years thinking everything was their fault. But it wasn't. It isn't. We do each other a supreme disservice when we throw guilt on another person. We should instead be looking for ways to relieve one another of the burden of guilt and shame.

Hear me: it's not your fault. You don't deserve to live a life of self-punishment, writhing in bitterness. God has a plan for you—a plan to prosper you, to give you hope, and to give you a future (Jeremiah 29:11).

God's intention for us is *goodness*. He doesn't want his children walking around looking like they're chewing on lemons. He wants us to hold on to him as our ultimate hope when things get tough. And hope alleviates the weight of guilt. Hope empowers us to live with sunshine radiating through us even when it rains. When people look at us, they should experience God and all the joy and blessing he bestows upon us.

Why do we insist on living like lemon chewers?

If someone were to tell you to take all your pain, roll it up into a ball, and throw it at the sun, and by doing so you would receive immeasurable joy, would you not immediately begin balling up your pain? Would you not throw it as hard and as far as you could?

I love that God takes our affliction and turns it into joy.

And that joy—which is more dynamic and much deeper than happiness—allows us to heal.

Receive God's healing today. I believe that his healing can be instant and even overwhelming to experience. We need only ask for it. Remember Job. If you are suffering from bitterness or loss or pain at this very moment, I challenge you to set down this book, get on your knees, and cry out to God. He's big enough to hear your disappointment and pain. He's big enough to carry you when you cannot walk. He's big enough to absorb your disillusionment and hurt. Just give it to him; cry out to see his face and receive your healing.

Let me add one more thing to the thought of receiving your healing. You may be reading this book right now and saying to yourself, "But it was my fault that my child died" or "It was my fault that I injured that person." You may even be thinking that you deserve to face the punishment of everlasting shame and guilt.

Let me tell you something, my friend: get rid of that false guilt.

Trust in God and his plan for you. Accept his strength. Stand up, receive your healing, and praise God in the midst of thinking that it was your fault.

Understand this: we serve a good God! And he doesn't want you sitting around taking the blame for something he allowed to happen. I know you may not understand what I'm saying, but I have been there before, and I have let God have all of those anxious thoughts. I've been healed, and today it's your turn.

Please repeat this prayer out loud:

> God,
>
> I'm sorry for anything I've done to take the glory from you. I need you to heal me right now. In your Holy Scriptures, you say, "Thy will be done in earth, as it is in heaven."
>
> Your Word also tells me in Isaiah 55:8–9:
>
> "For my thoughts are not your thoughts,
>   neither are your ways my ways,"
>   declares the LORD.
> "As the heavens are higher than the earth,
>   so are my ways higher than your ways
>   and my thoughts than your thoughts."
>
> I've been hurting for quite a while now and I need you to touch my spirit and revive me today. Please, loving Father, take the pain, guilt, and shame away from me. Allow me to forgive myself for my past experiences.

I love you, I'm healed, and I leave it all in your hands.

In Jesus' name,

Amen.

ACCEPT THE POWER OF COMMUNITY

I believe there is a significant step to moving on from pain that most people don't recognize the importance of: get past your sufferings to the point that you are able to love and serve others who need you in their own times of trouble.

I've learned that you should always treat others as you would have them treat you. When Christian passed away and my family began the grieving and healing process, there were many people who comforted us and offered to help in any way they could. These same people were going through pain as well—they knew and loved Christian. Even in the midst of their own grief for our son they were still able to express compassion and comfort.

Truth be told, without the aid of friends and family, without their support and comfort and prayers, my family would not have been able to make it through. I firmly believe that.

People told us, "I have no concept of the pain you are going through, but I am here for you." People would just sit with us and *be* with us—people who'd known us for many years, who had been at college with me, who had flown into town to be with us. People who had mentored my wife and me. They all came and said, "You don't have to say anything. We just want to *be* with you so you know we are here if you need us." Just like Job's friends who sat with him for seven days in silence and simply mourned with him—that's what we experienced.

Their offering of companionship through the darkest hell my family ever experienced was like an open door for us to experience the deep love and affection that God has for us. What a beautiful act of love—people trying not to say anything that was unnatural, but simply being there for us when we couldn't stand on our own. They moved everything off their schedules to come and cook for us and do our laundry and clean our house and make sure our kids were able to carry on with school. What a blessing.

The people who knew us the best didn't have to ask us for permission to help us and comfort us. I didn't have to text or call someone to pick up food for us. And it wasn't only adults who served us in our need. Randall II's friends, who helped carry Christian's casket, came over and helped out and did whatever they could to comfort us. That was beautiful.

The help and love and comfort we received during our time of grief showed me how important it is to treat others as you would hope to be treated. It was a beautiful reminder that when my friends and family and church family need help and comfort, I can provide the kind of love that God gives to me and that I received in my time of need.

We need to think about others first. We can't get so involved with ourselves that we forget there are those close to us who are hurting. We need to be cognizant of others' needs. And let's face it: we can all be selfish. I was so selfish at one point in my life that I was afraid to do things that would take me out of my comfort zone. For instance, I was afraid to shake the hand of somebody in a wheelchair. Silly, I know. But we all have phobias and things that make us feel uncomfortable. "Don't make me do anything that's going to push me out of my comfort zone," we say. But being there for others can't be one of those phobias.

We need to be others-oriented. We need to be caring toward those who need it. We need to be okay with stepping into other people's problems. If we can get out of our own little worlds, then we can actually be saints to someone. There are many people around us who need our love and good deeds. When we are others-oriented we look for ways to make someone else's life better.

I have a friend named Chester who attends our church along with his wife, Gloria. Chester's around seventy years old and is the type of guy who can make you laugh just by the sound of his voice—you know what's coming when Chester's around!

Chester served in our military and has been through a lot. He's always in pain because his body has been through the ringer, and he has to take pain medication constantly. But I know, without a shadow of a doubt, that I'm Chester's pastor. He calls me about three or four times a week. When we talk he makes me laugh so much. I return the favor and we laugh together. He's the kind of guy that if you call him or stop by or say hi to him, he acts like he won the lottery. He's so appreciative when I reach out to him.

I think my relationship with Chester is the kind of relationship we should seek to cultivate with others. I don't only call Chester when something's wrong, and he doesn't only call me when he needs prayer for something or when he's not doing well. I call him just to tell him I love him and to thank him for encouraging me the way he does. I hold Chester in high regard because I know he holds me in high regard. He considers me a family member. He tells me stories of when he used to play football (and to this day I don't think Chester ever played football!). He says to me, "Boy, if I'd have played in your day, I'd a took you down!" And we laugh some more.

We should all want to be as encouraging as Chester.

Being others-oriented is good for everyone, and I think it's demanded of everyone as well. Too often we forget that we are to befriend the lonely or feed the person on the street who has no food. We forget that we are supposed to shelter those with no place to stay. I think we fail to help others because we don't want to become part of their problems. But we better the world when we take the time to visit a senior citizen who has no one to visit her or who is struggling through dementia. We brighten our world when we take a meal to someone experiencing the loss of a family member or a family experiencing the joy of a new baby.

We are in this life together. So why not help one another? Because in the end, helping others helps *you*. It enriches your life and moves you past your own hurts—especially if you're working through the process of grieving and moving on. When you're focused on others you're not dwelling on yourself. And that's a win-win situation.

CHAPTER 8
REFLECTION QUESTIONS

*How do you handle emotional or spiritual pain? Are you an
internal or external griever? Why do you think you're that way?*

━━

*Do you tend to hold on to grief, or are you able to let it
go in the appropriate season? Would you say your way of
handling grief is a healthy one? How so, or not so?*

━━

*Think of a time when a difficult situation brought
on grief. How hard was it to reach out to God? Did
you feel alone or comforted by him? Explain.*

━━

*Have you ever felt so guilty for being a part of a difficult
situation that you were unable to let go of blame? If so,
what helped you overcome that feeling? Or have you
helped someone let go of guilt and blame? How?*

━━

*The saying goes that grief makes you stronger. Has
that been true in your experience? How has it changed
your relationship with God? With others?*

━━

How important is community to your ability to deal with grief?

━━

PRINCIPLE 5

RUNNING THE TWO-MINUTE DRILL

KEEP LIFE ON ITS HEELS

To succeed . . . you need to find something to hold on to, something to motivate you, something to inspire you.

—TONY DORSETT

Whenever I took the field for a game I always wanted to dictate the rhythm and pace. I wanted us to go out as if it were just another practice, and the pressure to play was normal and not overwhelming. If I was levelheaded and at ease, executing my own assignments and working my best to help the process by running the offense smoothly, our team would then respond with the same confidence.

But as I'm sure you know, football is a game of momentum and emotion. The game can change in a flash: a blocked punt, a sack, a forced fumble, an interception, or a kickoff return for a touchdown. If any of these things happens, a team can be thrown off its rhythm and game plan or it can be infused with passion and extreme focus because the momentum has shifted their way.

In life, my personality mirrored the way in which I sought to lead my team on the field: even-tempered, not wanting to rattle anyone, at peace. But life is not a static endeavor. Though there's the grinding-it-out aspect to it—just like in football—there are also the highs and lows.

You make the first-string high school football team. Momentum swing!

You graduate with honors from college. Kickoff return for a touchdown!

You get married. Ninety-nine-yard quarterback draw for a touchdown—and the crowd goes wild!

You lose your job. Sack.

You find out your best friend lied to you. Fumble.

Your spouse admits to an affair. Interception.

It seems a bit crude to relate these football terms to life, but I do it to show you the dynamic nature of life and to remind you—and me!—that there are times in our lives that force us to alter things a bit and make us adjust our game plan.

When I would run the two-minute drill at the end of a game, I had to dictate the pace to the other team, keeping them on their heels in order to win the game.

The two-minute drill is exhilarating, but it also demands precision: precision in your passing, in your play calling, in your reading of the defense, and in your execution. The room for error is small. If you mismanage the clock or fail to convert on fourth down, you're done.

Nowadays, many NFL and college teams tend to open the game with a two-minute drill. It's their attempt to dictate the momentum of what will happen. It's like kick-starting your offense to keep the defense guessing and unbalanced.

Most quarterbacks can run a two-minute drill. Some, however, are experts at it. Peyton Manning can run the two-minute offense with so much precision and confidence that coaches predicate their offense on the no-huddle format. He's an expert at it—it jives with his skill set.

Sometimes life demands the two-minute drill. Perhaps it's a project that has to be done in a small window of time. Or maybe it's a chance that will never come again so you must be at your very best to take advantage of the opportunity. There is high risk but high reward. Other times demand the two-minute drill just to get you out of the doldrums or to get your mind off your hurt and onto the task at hand: living.

In general, a two-minute drill is for those times when you have to pick up the tempo in life and take over in a situation as a leader. Many people fear those situations that demand a certain amount of changeup, a certain amount of fearless leadership, because they feel they are not called to be a leader. There are others who are called but lack the maturity to go out and dictate the pace—take the bull by the horns, to quote the cliché—and make something happen when it absolutely needs to.

In life, however, you don't need to be a Peyton Manning to run a change-up life plan. You just need to be able to see the light ahead—the light that tells you, "It's okay. Yes, it's been hard, but if you just get up and get going today, you can change things up."

A TIME FOR EVERYTHING

Just like in football, in life "there is a time for everything, and a season for every activity under the heavens" (Ecclesiastes 3:1). There's a time to be patient and grind it out, and there's a time to pick up the pace and get your juices flowing so that you can kick-start your mind and heart and move on from hurt.

When I had to rehab my knee I had to be patient. It was a tough, slow time. When initially my knee felt stronger, I wanted to try running again and even making cuts. But the doctors warned me, "Yes, Randall, you can run, but don't cut to the right or left. Just run straight." So, though I wanted to start running like my old self, I had to be patient and stay the course. I had to take time to become stronger. If I pushed it too much, my knee might cave under the pressure and give out and I would have to undergo surgery again.

Finally, after six months the doctors gave me the okay to begin running and cutting like normal—I could finally see the light at the end of the tunnel. But I was unsure of myself, cleared to play physically but mentally not quite out of the woods yet. I needed a little security. So I used my Orthotech Performer knee brace. It kept my leg sturdy and allowed me to be a little more risky. It stabilized me and gave me confidence that I wouldn't reinjure myself.

When Christian passed, it was one of the most difficult times of my life. But I had to power through it with my family. I am still, several years later, not completely done with the grieving process, but I see the light at the end of the tunnel. I actually saw a bit of that light right after he passed, knowing that he was with God and in a better place. And that gave me the peace I needed to deal with losing my beautiful little boy.

The point here is that in the midst of my trial I kept my faith because I had hope, and that allowed me to see the end game, just like having that knee brace instilled within me a confidence to be my best self on the playing field.

In all this there is motion: a forward mobility. Like when my doctor told me that I couldn't cut to the left or to the right but could still run straight. Even that was a big part of my knee's healing process—just keeping it moving straight.

It is the same in life. Whether it is recognizing that we need to set a peaceful pace to keep balance in life or whether we understand that we need to infuse our life with a two-minute drill in order to kick-start our emotions and life, we are always playing the game of life, always moving forward. That is important to realize.

There is also the idea of a light drawing us forward—that light of hope when gloom is our only friend, that light of faith that prods us forward and strengthens us when we need to be patient and grind things out. There is a time for everything, and each moment propels us forward.

STOP THINKING THAT YOU'RE IN CONTROL

I was able to make a full recovery from that surgery. My knee, to this day, feels as good as it ever has. But some players never recover from those types of injuries. Likewise, there are some people who never recover from personal tragedy.

I think many fail to recover from tragedy in life for the same reason some guys never recover from surgery: we want to take things into our own hands, do things our way instead of the way that best suits our needs. We think that we can manipulate a situation, as if we have total control. But who are we kidding? We control very little. And yet we live like we control everything.

When tragedy strikes, don't be in a hurry to get out of that situation. Don't be in a hurry to forget about it, glossing over the very thing you need to deal with. God gives us these situations, just like he did with Job, so that we can learn and grow from them. He wants us to know him on a deeper level and plumb the depths of his mind to discover the reasons and lessons he has for us. If we try to jump out of the trial too early we may not discover what God wants to teach us.

The irony is that many times when we think we've jumped out of the trial, the reality is we stay in it longer. We remain hurt and bruised and disillusioned because we were not patient enough to learn and exit the trial when we should have, according to God's plan.

So the result is there are many people walking around in life with all these trials stuck to their hearts—pains they've never dealt with correctly. Why can't we learn to be patient when our pain wracks us?

When we fail to deal with our junk we can also become accustomed to it. Some people end up "liking" or "thriving" on pain and bask in the trials they carry around. It's as if some people would rather stay on pain medicine than find true healing. Because we want to be in control, we would rather listen to a doctor than to God. We'd rather treat a symptom than heal the disease.

It's difficult to release control. I get that. But the ramifications of not releasing can be grave. On the other hand, when we do let go and practice patience God's plan finds us right where it should: waiting on him. Abiding.

Pastor and author Tullian Tchividjian recently wrote on suffering in his book *Glorious Ruin: How Suffering Sets You Free*. In an interview he gave shortly after the book's release, he outlined what suffering did for him:

God used the crucible of suffering to disillusion me about who I was. The pain cleared my vision, and once it was taken away, I realized just how much I'd been relying on the endorsement of others to make me feel like I mattered. I had turned personal validation into my primary source of meaning and value (what theologians call the basis of my self-justification), so that without it I was miserable and depressed. I had made something good—the approval and admiration of others—into an idol.[1]

It's good to be stripped of the things that make us into idol worshippers. But we won't discover what those things are if we, in our brash and controlling way, sidestep the process of pain. As we abide in God, it may be uncomfortable, but it's necessary so that we will finally emerge to be the people he wants us to be.

Pastor Tchividjian told us what we don't want to hear but what I think we inherently know:

God did not rescue me out of the pain; He rescued me through the pain! Indeed, I had to learn the hard way (the only way?) that the gospel alone can free us from our addiction to being liked—that Jesus measured up for us so that we wouldn't have to live under

the enslaving pressure of measuring up for others—
including ourselves.[2]

God says he will not give us more than we can bear (1 Corinthians 10:13). He's not going to allow trials to enter our lives
that we cannot handle. The key here is to always look for God
when the circumstance flares up. The problem is too often that
we can't take our eyes away from our pain long enough to see
that God is walking beside us offering to carry the load for us.
When I walked into the hospital the day Christian passed away,
God was carrying me; that's really the only way I know how to
explain it.

It's the same thing with blessings. Some people desire to
become multimillionaires, thinking if they can achieve that
level of financial success then they won't have to worry about
paying bills and their kid's college education and their mort-
gage or car payment. But here's the thing: God's also not going
to give us more than we can handle financially, because what
happens is people find financial success and then think they no
longer need God.

So the concept about not getting more than we can bear in
life relates not only to the pain and toil of this life but also to
the blessings. We need to keep that in mind when we are praying for prosperity and for deliverance. It's like Pastor Tchividjian

said—God is not going to save us out of our pain; he's going to save us through it.

I don't know about you, but I need God every day! I need him in my finances. I need him in my worship. I need him when I'm studying the Scriptures preparing for a sermon. I need him when I'm angry. I need him when I'm happy. I need him when I'm seeking him to find solutions to a problem in life. I need him in my relationships with my kids and my wife. I need him in everything I do. He *has* to be the center point of life. I believe, with all my heart, that when God is the center, then we will be able to see the light at the end of the tunnel.

ABUNDANT LIFE

I always tell people—be it my student athletes or the great folks in my church—that the sky is the limit. I believe that we should put our minds to the task of being perfect just as God is perfect. This is our goal—and we are instructed and challenged to pursue his perfection (Matthew 5:48). When we do strive for this perfection, I think we will finally begin to understand and experience the good things God has for us.

I don't think there are limitations to what God can do for us. I do, however, believe that there are limitations—self-imposed limitations—to what we do with what God gives us.

But here's the great thing about God: he says that he has great plans for us. Plans to prosper us. That means we don't stay in the same state of life; we have the afterlife ahead of us. We go on to a life void of pain and sorrow; our tears are wiped away when finally we meet God in heaven. That's the ultimate glory, the ultimate perfection. But we can experience a small portion of that glory and perfection here on earth if we would just be patient in our suffering and our toil, wait for his perfect time, and believe that he has great things planned for us.

Living a life with great anticipation demands a strong faith, and it's that very faith that empowers us to lay down the things that would weigh us down or stand before us, deterring us from our goal. That goal is to live in God's glory and to experience the abundant life he offers to us each day. This life is not about building up our own glory. Rather, it is all about pursuing God and realizing our life as it stands in relation to him. What a sobering thought!

But be careful here. Don't hear me say we need to wait on God and then do nothing in this life. If we claim to have faith in God but our actions reveal a lack of faith, then we should expect very little from God because we are not willing to trust him and live out our faith with the everyday things in life. Conversely, if we say we have faith and we exercise that faith through our actions, then watch out, because God loves moving when his children move. And that's when the sky becomes our limit. We need to be vigilant to keep our faith focused on him and not the *things* that might come from faith.

I heard a saying growing up that went like this: "Baseball, hot dogs, apple pie, and Chevrolet." Apparently those things were the end-all, be-all. As if life revolved around those things or was complete when we possessed them. But that saying limits your view of what is actually attainable in life.

Our culture says that if we attain these staples in life (and you can fill in the blank with whatever you want—maybe for you it's soccer, tacos, chocolate cake, and Mercedes), then we've made it. Now I'm not suggesting those things are intrinsically bad. I like apple pie! But that outlook on life sets a person up for failure because it presents a limited view. It takes our perception of success and places it in man's hands instead of at God's feet, where it belongs. Once we fail and don't achieve these limited things, we point the finger at God and say things like, *Life is unfair! I did everything right and this is all I got?* When we set our sights on the things of this world we will always be left wanting more.

Not so when we engage a heavenly perspective on life. We could never point our finger at God, because when we align our wills and desires with what God wants for us, we are saying we trust him no matter what—like Job. That no matter what tragedy befalls us or what success we attain, it is all God's.

It's when things go wonky on us that we tend to point our finger, assigning blame for our lack of success. But that's because we've placed our hopes and dreams in things that, though they can to a certain degree be measured, ultimately wither and die. They are temporal. The temporal will never fully satisfy us.

I would summarize all this by saying that God's will is victorious, whereas man's will sets us up for failure. It's so easy to fall into the trap of frustration and think we are no better than our worst failure. And when that happens we say, "How can I do what God wants me to do when I can't even succeed at hot dogs and Chevrolet?" That's exactly where the enemy wants us: failing God and failing ourselves, yet still believing we need to do things our own way. That pathway leads only to selfishness, disappointment, and pride.

There is an easy way to keep our focus, yet few consistently implement this handy little tool: goal setting.

THE IMPORTANCE OF SETTING GOALS

At some point in this life we will all set a goal. Whether it's an educational one, a vocational one, or even a relational one, we all set them. Goals are good. They help us stay focused and run the race of life with purpose.

When I coach my track team, the Nevada Gazelles, we

don't necessarily race against each other or even other opponents. Rather, we race against the clock—we race against the top times in each track-and-field discipline. That time stamp stands as our goal. Our team runs or jumps or throws with the purpose of beating that time or distance. The goal gives our athletes purpose.

I think there are two things we should remember as we approach life and everything we will encounter, be it good or bad.

First, in life everything is attainable as long as it aligns with God's will. If we teach our young people this at a young age it will free them to run the race of life with confidence, unafraid to fail because they know they are running life's race for God and to please him. They will endure hardships with the same grace and elegance with which they celebrate victory. They will live content knowing their pathway is determined and protected by God. What freedom!

Second, our mind-set needs to be grounded in the eternal character of God. Our eternal God has no beginning, no end, and no limits to what he can do. When my son and daughters get ready to perform the high jump at a track meet, I tell them that we have no limitations. I try to free their minds of their physical limitations and the doubts that arise in all athletes when they compete. Likewise, just as God never slows down or loses strength, I tell my whole track team that to distinguish themselves and win, they need to be at their strongest on the last lap. Most athletes will weaken during the last lap; but if they train themselves to give their strongest burst at that point in the race, then they won't only beat the competition; they'll do so handily.

I tell Randall II, Vashti, and Grace (my second-youngest daughter) not to aim at the bar they are trying to jump over. Rather, I tell them to aim eight inches above the bar. So just in case their foot drags a bit, they'll still make the jump. If they merely aimed at the bar and they dragged their foot, they would knock the bar off and miss their jump.

Another trick I teach them when they compete is to come into a meet at a higher level than what the others are jumping. If, for example, the common clearance for Randall II's age group is six feet two inches, I tell him to come into the meet at six feet five inches.

Recently, Randall II began gunning for the national record of seven feet and one-half inch for his age group. As we trained together I told him his goal was not seven feet and three quarters of an inch, but seven feet two inches.

At a recent meet Randall II came into the jumps planning on jumping at least eight jumps with a personal goal of seven feet two. He started low with everyone else at six feet four. Everyone else failed at that height. Randall II, however, made that jump and the next several jumps. And by the time he reached his goal of seven feet two, he had set a new national AAU record in the intermediate division. He then aimed at seven three. He missed those jumps, but the point is that he set his goal, trained for his goal, and then achieved his goal.

Some people, however, set their goals too low. I believe this happens because people set their goals based on what others are achieving. But setting your goals according to someone else's standards limits you. You should never set your goal based on what others are achieving.

Growing up I was always told to never forget where I came from, especially if I found success. Well, I succeeded in life; I pursued my dream of becoming an NFL quarterback. And then a friend told me to beware the crab-in-the-bucket scenario. The crab-in-the-bucket scenario is basically this: If you set high goals for yourself and you go out and achieve those goals you'll find success. But when you return home you may have a hard time with some of the folks who never thought you'd amount to anything, especially at such a high level. So when you reach out to try and help someone from your past they may actually pull you down, like one crab in a bucket reaching up to hold on to the crab that is out of the bucket.

It's a sad reality, but sometimes we can't see beyond the front door in terms of what we think is possible for our lives.

That mind-set must change also. The sky is the limit! We can't live our lives like the servant from the biblical parable whose boss gave him a talent to use and invest, but he was scared and hid it in the ground.

Our goals must not be based in mediocrity or fear. Instead they should be based on what God has placed in our hearts. So many of us hear those whisperings in our hearts and actually fear them or refuse to believe that God could be placing them in our hearts. We tell ourselves we don't seem to be equipped for the task.

That's *exactly* the task we should undertake—the one that is impossible without the help and strength of God in our lives. Mediocre goals are a result of too much looking around at what the competition is doing and not on what burns within our hearts.

Don't look around at what the world constantly bombards you with regarding what is acceptable or what is attainable. You need to run the race of life with an inner time clock, an inner goal that no one sees. That needs to be your sole measurement— a measurement that comes from God.

I remember hearing the story about how Michael Phelps's coach keeps Michael razor-sharp. In one training session, Phelps's coach actually cracked Michael's goggles, which would obviously allow water in and blur his vision. But that coaching method prepared Phelps for the Beijing Olympics, in which

Phelps accidentally cracked his goggles while diving in for the two-hundred-meter race. Immediately Phelps's goggles began to fill up. But it didn't matter. His coach trained him not on what other swimmers were doing but on what time Phelps had to beat—usually his own time. He also trained Phelps to count strokes in accordance with the time he needed to beat. So when his goggles began filling up with water Phelps swam undeterred. He simply counted his strokes and set out to beat the goal that only he knew. It didn't matter what the others swimmers were doing; it only mattered what Phelps was doing. In an interview Phelps told the sports announcer that he knew if he beat his goal, he'd beat everyone in the pool.

When God lays something on your heart and you feel the burning to go and do it, you must trust him that he will equip you to accomplish it. Phelps swam with unfazed confidence. He relied on his intense training and trusted it when it mattered most.

When you encounter an obstacle in life—when your goggles begin to fill up—what will you do? Will you pull up in your swim lane and scream foul play? Or will you continue on, relying on God to carry you through?

I think you know the best answer. Embrace your life, your dreams, your goals. Center them on God. Set your pace. And go for it!

CHAPTER 9
REFLECTION QUESTIONS

When facing difficult situations, are you able to focus on the light at the end of the tunnel? Or do you find yourself struggling to keep faith? What do you do to keep yourself moving forward? What do you need to do that you aren't?

———

Do you find it hard to step back and let God be in charge? Detail a time in your life when you wish you'd let him take over rather than handling things yourself. How might things have ended differently?

———

How good are you at setting goals? Do you achieve them? Are they the goals God wants you to focus on? Explain.

———

Detail a specific goal here. Now analyze it—is it set too high? Too low? Just right? Explain how you are going to meet that goal. Go for it!

———

PRINCIPLE 6
ABSORBING THE HITS

SPIRITUAL MATURITY BREEDS CONTENTMENT

Only in the darkness can you see the stars.

—MARTIN LUTHER KING JR.

One day after Christian's funeral and the memorial service, Felicity and I were sitting in our bedroom. We were looking at pictures, remembering our beautiful son. We didn't have answers to the lingering "why?" questions. We just had his memory and the massive void in our lives. Our son wasn't coming back. This was our reality. It hurt.

At that point in the process, healing stretches out into eternity—we wonder if we'll ever get there. It was all Felicity and I could do to take things one day at a time.

A month later Sherman—one of the ministers at our church—and his wife, Cynthia, called Felicity and me into a room at the church.

"We just want to talk with you two," Sherman said. "We want to tell you what God revealed to us about Christian's death."

"Okay," I said.

"Christian didn't die, like the reports said. Christian was called back home to be with the Father, and he made the choice to heed the voice of God."

Sherman went on to tell us that Christian didn't sneak out of the house like everyone else had thought. Rather, he heard God's voice outside and he followed it. He walked into the arms of his heavenly Father . . . then his body fell into the Jacuzzi. When his body fell into the water he was, at that point, like Enoch—already with God.

Now I know that some may read this and say, "Yeah, right, whatever." But the people who would say that do not value spiritual things the way Felicity and I do. We look for the spiritual in our everyday lives not just to encourage us but to recognize God's activity, his hand at work in everything that we set out to accomplish. We believe that God created this world and he governs it with a sovereign hand. We believe that nothing happens in this world—for good or for evil—outside of his will. Our view of God affects our view of the world and that goes for every person, whether you believe in God or not. Those who don't believe in God and can't understand why a supposedly good Creator would let a tragedy like this happen are shaped by their disbelief as much as we are shaped by our belief.

We viewed Sherman's story about Christian as God's hand at work in the grieving process. And in that hand we found not only deep comfort but peace as well. Felicity told me once she cried every day after losing Christian. Grief has a way of persuading a person to give in to unwarranted guilt. This revelation was one more opportunity to say, "Honey, it's going to be okay. It's not your fault. It was God's decision that this happened. It was no fault of ours."

Our faith tells us that God is the giver of life. He also takes life away. My family lives contented in this truth. But the outside world finds that hard to believe—even naive. Sometimes your faith can make grief lonely; it seems like it would be much easier to toss around blame and act out of pure, unadulterated emotion. But that is the lie that guilt and grief foster.

Another element to our faith manifests itself in the group of people—friends and family and our church—who surround us on a daily basis. When like-minded people surround us during one of the most difficult times in life, we see clearly the treasure of faith.

Life, however, can loom too large even for people of faith. I had people suggest during our ordeal that I take antidepressants for fear that I might succumb to depression. I didn't do it, though. And it's not because I'm some sort of superman. I believe that I've been fortunate enough to live in contentment with my God.

It's hard for me to explain to people, but the more at peace I am with what God has given me at a base level, the better I am able to roll with the ups and downs of life. I put so much stock in my faith that it seems counterproductive to me to use a foreign substance to help balance my mind. I'm not trying to diminish those who do use antidepressants out of a real and deep physiological need. I'm simply saying that for my family and me, we were fortunate enough to have a deep faith to cling to. And we continue to cling to it each and every day. Though we think about Christian on a daily basis, our faith makes it possible for us to carry on.

The nineteenth-century Scottish pastor George MacDonald said, "We can walk without fear, full of hope and courage and strength, waiting for the endless good which God is always giving as fast as he can get us to take it in." That's what we cling to—the endless good that God gives to us. He offers it; we need only reach out and accept it.

STEP BY STEP

I shared Sherman's story with our day-care minister, Charlene Neves. She was Christian's teacher, so she had special ties to Christian and was deeply affected by his passing. After I told her what Sherman had communicated to us, she said, "Wow, that's amazing. The day Christian died I saw a bright light in your backyard—the light was coming from heaven. I know it was the light of God."

As you can imagine, I perked up when I heard Charlene tell us of the vision she saw in our backyard. It coincided with Sherman's story, making it more evident to me that God was at work to ease our pain by giving us a glimpse into what he was up to.

If Charlene's story wasn't enough, there was Mama Jean's story. Mama Jean was in a rehabilitation facility. She had gone through surgery and had a few setbacks. She told me that she had actually flatlined two times while in the hospital, yet had been revived. It was a miracle she was alive. Mama Jean asked me to come see her, so I did.

When I reached the care facility I found Mama Jean bright-eyed in her room.

"Pastor, I need to tell you something."

"Okay, Mama Jean. What's up?"

"You know I've flatlined twice this year. After this last time, while recuperating, I had a dream that I went to heaven. As I began walking around I saw Christian—he was there in heaven. He was a little taller than he was when he passed away. It was such a wonderful sight.

"I called out to him and waved. 'Christian,' I said, 'Christian, come on. Let's go!' But Christian said that he was fine where he was and that he was home, where he was supposed to be."

What an incredible blessing that story was for Felicity and me! These stories from Mama Jean, Charlene, and Sherman were not made up. They were experiences that God gave to each of them so they could tell us. These stories gave us a sense of godly peace. They've also helped us and others to get through a difficult time of grief. Those stories aided my wife and me in our spiritual maturity.

God says that our ways are not his ways (Isaiah 55:8). God's ways are so much higher than ours. But the Bible also says that when we make a decision to become children of God, we then have the mind of Christ (1 Corinthians 2:16). So, on the one hand, God's ways are not our ways. But on the other hand, we have the mind of Christ. It's an interesting paradox. We will never understand God fully in this age or maybe even the age to come, but because we have the mind of Christ (for those who believe in him) we are able to discern his ways and what they mean in our lives.

I think that inside of each believer lies latent spiritual insight—a spiritual giftedness if you will. It takes a stirring to occur in order for us to tap into that gifting. I see those stories that came to us from our trusted friends as catalyst moments in my faith and Felicity's as well. It took us to a whole new level of spiritual maturity. And if I think hard on it, those stories actually took us to another level of gratitude. We were learning how to be thankful, how to lay stuff down—how to lay down the thoughts of why this tragedy happened to Christian. So those stories helped mature us in the aspect of wondering what happened to Christian. We were set free and given a new portal into our faith.

Like any trial that comes into our lives, the surrounding events and the words from friends regarding Christian were character building for us. We knew that God cared enough for us to give us these special words from our friends. And so we would continue to trust him. We were confident that God would continue to provide for us spiritually; we just needed to do what was required to aid in the constant building of our relationship with him.

FINDING CONTENTMENT

Have you ever thought about what it means to be *satisfied* with where you are in life, while at the same time failing to be *content*?

I can be satisfied with a million dollars. But God wants me to be content with food, shelter, and clothing. It's only when we understand what it means to be content in our lives that we will understand how to handle the good things life brings our way. When those things do happen to us we can be grateful, content.

When Christian came into our lives he was a healthy and strong twenty-two-inch-long baby who weighed 9 pounds and 13 ounces. I was grateful. My wife and kids were grateful. He was our little blessing, and we lived in a state of thankfulness for him. My perspective, when he was with us, was one of blessing—*God has given me this child, so I will be forever grateful*. I could be grateful because I was already content in my life. I saw my life as a glass completely full—all the added bonuses of love and adoration from my growing family just made me spill over.

The strength of my contentment allowed me to remain grateful even after Christian was taken from us. That's what contentment does for all of us. It allows us to accept the good things *and* the bad things in this life with the same amount of grace. And that, my friends, is only possible through God.

The flipside to this is discontent. When we're satisfied yet always wanting more, we waver in the good and the bad. We're not thankful for what has been given to us, so when something bad happens or that blessing of money is taken away, we crack. It's not so easy when we lose our job or our spouse leaves us or our son dies. That's when life crystallizes and we see the world through a new set of lenses. How will we respond to what we see?

Many people, when they go through a tough time, tend to get angry. I think it's part of our natural proclivity to get mad when tragedy strikes. That's our carnal mind screaming out, "Unfair, unfair." But when we look at what Scripture says, we learn this:

> Those who live according to the flesh have their minds set on what the flesh desires; but those who live in accordance with the Spirit have their minds set on what the Spirit desires. The mind governed by the flesh is death, but the mind governed by the Spirit is life and peace. The mind governed by the flesh is

hostile to God; it does not submit to God's law, nor can it do so. Those who are in the realm of the flesh cannot please God. (Romans 8:5–8)

When we're content in who we are in God, we'll remain content when trouble comes our way. Contentment allows us to see the world the same at all times and accept what comes our way. It's not always going to be easy, but a contented heart doesn't require it to be. A contented heart looks down the road with anticipation and vigor, ready for what is to come, no matter what it is, and rests in the peace that the present holds wisdom for the coming trials.

Let me add here that you don't have to experience a life-altering trial to come to a saving knowledge of Jesus. You can enter into a relationship with him when things are going great. When the trials do come, however, they engender a certain level of gratitude within your faith.

I know some reading this book might ask, "Wasn't there a time during the tragedy of your son's death that you got mad and questioned your faith in God?"

I would say no.

I don't apologize for saying no. But you must understand that's where I was and still am in my life, in my faith. I don't ever want to second-guess the One who created me. I didn't create myself. And it's only through his grace that we were able to produce a child. God was the author of all of that.

When I originally thought about writing this book, I wanted the title to be *He Was His First*. Meaning that Christian, like Adam in the Bible, was brought forth by the will of God. Therefore he, our baby boy, was God's first. God knitted Christian; he fashioned him inside my wife's womb. He made him into who he was supposed to be on this earth. And when I think about that truth it makes it that much easier to look back upon those stories that our friends told us and see the Creator's hand at work. Of course it makes sense that God would take Christian home—Christian was his first!

Believing in God's will demands that we find complete peace in God—in how he's cared for us through blessing and how he teaches us through trial. In *both*, we should strive for contentment.

CHAPTER 10
REFLECTION QUESTIONS

*What do you see as the difference between being
satisfied and content? How do you think the
world and media would define them?*

———

Be honest with yourself: Are you content, *or are you
only* satisfied? *Does your satisfaction/contentment come
from personal fulfillment or from God? Explain.*

———

*Describe a time when life was tough but you realized you
were okay with it. How were you able to remain content?*

———

*What does George MacDonald's phrase "the endless
good that God gives to us" mean to you personally?*

———

CONCLUSION
LAYING IT DOWN

ADJUST FOR ANY SITUATION

The boy who is going to make a great man must not make up his mind merely to overcome a thousand obstacles, but to win in spite of a thousand repulses and defeats.

—THEODORE ROOSEVELT

One Sunday after I had finished preaching, one of the sisters came up to me after church. This woman was real, standing before me. But her words were not from this world. To this day I believe them to be angelic.

"Pastor," she said, "your wife's womb is blessed."

Okay, I thought. I didn't know what to think or even how to respond.

What do you say to a statement like that? It was strange, completely unsolicited. So I brushed it off because I just couldn't believe what she was saying.

"Yeah, cool," I responded. "Go tell her that."

I played off the comment because I had no space for it in my brain. The woman left. But as I stood there greeting people and shaking hands I thought about her statement again. What did she mean, Felicity's womb was blessed?

I didn't know it at the time, but much like Mary and Elizabeth were informed ahead of time that they would have babies in the near future, we were receiving prophecy that we were to have another child.

Now before you blow your top, I'm not suggesting that my wife was going to miraculously conceive a messiah-baby. I'm just saying that the woman was using familiar terminology to tell us that we were going to have another baby.

After church I found Felicity and asked her if the lady had come to her.

"Yeah," she said. "She told me my womb was blessed."

Crazy, right? Well, it gets even crazier. That week Felicity bought a pregnancy test. It was positive! We were going to have a baby.

Keep in mind that I was forty-eight years old at the time, and Felicity had just turned forty-four. We had no intention of having additional children.

As I'm writing this book, Sophia, our third girl, is eight months old. How's that for blowing your mind? Well, if your mind's not blown, mine certainly was at the time. I thought, *Man, people are going to think we're trying to have a baby to replace Christian. How is this pregnancy going to go? It's high risk! Felicity and I are both in our forties, for crying out loud. What in the world are we going to do?*

Talk about needing to lay it down!

The truth of the matter was that we did not plan to have another child; it wasn't on our minds. But God, again, encouraged us through the words of man—in this specific case this woman in our church who told us we were going to have a baby. When we announced it to the church the congregation was overjoyed. We all went crazy in a good way.

I remember when Sister Maggie Santiago, Pastor Efrin's wife, told us that this baby was *not* to replace Christian. I had no idea what that meant. Well, we never asked the doctors to tell us the sex of our children during our pregnancies, and with Sophia we did the same. When she was born we understood what Maggie's words meant. We had another girl! What would she be like? What blessings would she bring into our lives? Something different from Christian, certainly. Christian was Christian. Sophia is Sophia. We had to let go of Christian. But we gained Sophia. And in receiving her into our lives, our family has more fully understood the give and take of blessings and trials, and that each brings with it a deepening of our faith in all aspects of our lives.

I remember, in particular, the day that Sophia Marie Ruth Cunningham was born. We were in the hospital, and I was feeding Felicity ice chips as she endured her contractions. But at one point I became overwhelmed with the situation. I looked at her and said, "Honey, what are we doing? I'm forty-eight. You're forty-four. We're not supposed to have any more children—we're too old for this. We're going to look like grandparents when our child graduates from high school."

Yet even as I uttered those words I felt God's peace on our lives. This pregnancy was part of his plan. He had this. Felicity and I just needed to remain faithful and be at peace with this tremendous blessing.

ABLE TO ENDURE

As I look back to some of the things that have happened in my life I can truly say that God is real. He grows us and matures us his way.

I grew up in Santa Barbara, a free-spirited environment. I moved to Las Vegas to attend UNLV. We all know what Vegas is about. You go there hoping to hit the big one and become rich, only to be deceived into losing your shirt. I then moved to Philadelphia thinking I was going to be the next greatest thing since sliced bread, only to find out that I was a prideful individual and that I needed mentors to groom me in my relationship with God.

Back in Vegas I was to find out that humility is the key to receiving exaltation in my relationship with my Creator. After that I was afforded the opportunity to learn about redemption in a purple Vikings uniform. Playing for Minnesota was a turnaround time in my life. My faith increased through learning how to trust God to lead me, even when being placed on the bench at the height of my career.

Playing for the Dallas Cowboys in 2000 really taught me about the calling on my life to disciple others. And my time in Baltimore as a Raven grew me as a leader. I enjoyed playing for Coach Billick and with the Ravens. I was healthy. I was having fun. But I knew, at that point, that I was sent to Baltimore for a greater purpose. There was a treasure to be mined there, and it wasn't just finishing off my career with the Ravens.

When I arrived in Baltimore I approached Ray Lewis and Rod Woodson, who had spent most of his career with the Steelers. I said, "You guys are the leaders of this team and I was wondering if I could go through this book, *The Man God Uses*, with you both. Would you commit to meeting with me for about a half hour each week?"

"Sure, we'll meet with you," they said. So we met that year each week. It was only one season but I was given that time with other leaders before I left the league.

Years later Rod called me up. He said, "Randall, I want to thank you for what you did in my life in 2001. I didn't understand what God was doing in my life back then. But thank you for pouring God's Word into my life, because now I do understand."

God allowed me to go through a year of not being able to play football to bring me back to the Vikings to take me down to Dallas, where I mentored some of my fellow players, and finally to take me to Baltimore so that I could have a positive impact in the lives of Ray and Rod and many other future leaders in the kingdom. What a humbling experience!

To this day I still hear from Ray. I pray for him. He's a true friend. Despite his schedule and status in the league, Ray's not a "too busy" guy. He takes my calls and we continue our relationship. *That*, my friend, is what life is all about. It's about connecting deeply with people, developing friendships, and giving of yourself.

It's amazing for me to think about how football started out as a vehicle for personal fulfillment in my life. But it ended as a way for me to find fulfillment in another more lasting way.

SEEING LIFE SIDEWAYS

We have to be able to see life sideways. What I mean by that is we can't always look at situations in life head-on and expect to understand the reasons they're happening. In order to look at something sideways, we must take time to see it from God's perspective. In each of my career situations, I was able to step back and readjust my purpose according to God's needs. And with his guidance I found opportunities for meaningful fulfillment—most especially in meeting the spiritual needs of some of the players with whom I worked.

For me, seeing life sideways is all about laying it down—laying down our preconceived notions, our own desires. Being in the moment and being okay with being in the moment. Such an attitude is only possible when we're steadfast in our faith in God. But with such an attitude, we can make it through any situation.

That's what aided me and Felicity and our family when tragedy struck. We try to live life with a spirit of openness to God's desires. For when you are open to your immediate circumstances, either good or bad, you aren't looking down the path of life wishing for more. Rather, you are looking around you at that specific moment in time. Your perspective does not skew. It remains unwavering.

It's the difference between an open hand and a clenched fist. One invites; the other rejects. One is able to lay down burdens; the other holds them tight.

How is your heart right now? Does it assume the posture of an open hand? Or is your heart clenched in anger and frustration because of what has happened to you or a loved one? At some point, you must open that fist, take what you hold on to so tightly, and lay it down. And when you do, you will find that though it might cause some temporary pain, it will also bring freedom. And freedom from pain, my friend, is a freedom straight from God.

What do you need to lay down today?

NOTES

CHAPTER 3
BRACING YOURSELF: DIG DEEP AND HOLD ON

1. C. S. Lewis, *A Grief Observed* (New York: HarperCollins, 1989), 48.

CHAPTER 4
MOVING TOWARD HOPE: CALLED TO SOMETHING MORE

1. Tony Dungy, *The Mentor Leader* (Wheaton, IL: Tyndale, 2010), 44.
2. This quote was taken from a sermon preached by Dr. Gordon Hugenberger of Park Street Church in Boston, Massachusetts.

CHAPTER 6
DOWN AT HALFTIME: PERSEVERANCE IN THE TOUGH TIMES

1. Timothy Keller, "Wisdom and Sabbath Rest," DenverPres.org, www.denverpres.org/sites/default/files/Wisdom_and_Sabbath_Rest.pdf.
2. Text taken from an Israeli travel brochure, written by a rabbi. As quoted in Gordon MacDonald, *Ordering Your Private World* (Nashville: Thomas Nelson, 2003), 201.
3. MacDonald, *Ordering Your Private World*, 196.

CHAPTER 9
RUNNING THE TWO-MINUTE DRILL: KEEP LIFE ON ITS HEELS

1. Josh Olds, "Interview with Tullian Tchividjian," LifeIsStory.com, November 20, 2012, www.lifeisstory.com/2012/11/interview-with-tullian-tchividjian/.
2. Tullian Tchividjian, *Glorious Ruin: How Suffering Sets You Free* (Colorado Springs: David C. Cook, 2012), 148–49.

Randall Cunningham, recipient of the NFL's Most Valuable Player Award, quarterbacked the Philadelphia Eagles and Minnesota Vikings and spent his final season with the Dallas Cowboys. He was voted to the NFL Pro Bowl four times. He is now a pastor and mentor in Las Vegas, Nevada.

WORTHY
PUBLISHING

IF YOU ENJOYED THIS BOOK, WILL YOU CONSIDER SHARING THE MESSAGE WITH OTHERS?

- Mention the book in a Facebook post, Twitter update, Pinterest pin, or blog post.

- Recommend this book to those in your small group, book club, workplace, and classes.

- Head over to facebook.com/worthypublishing, "LIKE" the page, and post a comment as to what you enjoyed the most.

- Tweet "I recommend reading #LayItDown by Randall Cunningham // @worthypub."

- Pick up a copy for someone you know who would be challenged and encouraged by this message.

- Write a review on amazon.com or bn.com.

You can subscribe to Worthy Publishing's
newsletter at www.worthypublishing.com.

WORTHY PUBLISHING   **WORTHY PUBLISHING**
FACEBOOK PAGE   **WEBSITE**